SPIRITUAL FREEDOM IN THE *BRAHMA SŪTRAS*

SPIRITUAL FREEDOM IN THE *BRAHMA SŪTRAS*

ॐ

CAROL PITTS

A facsimile edition of

The Concept of Spiritual Freedom in the Brahma Sūtras,

originally published in 1976.

Published by Mahodara Press

http://mywhatever.com/sanskrit/pitts

books@mywhatever.com

For publicity inquiries contact 213-394-5150

First facsimile edition, 2012

Book design for the facsimile edition by Les Morgan.

Cataloging data:

Spiritual Freedom in the Brahma Sūtras / A facsimile edition of: The Concept of Spiritual Freedom in the Brahma Sūtras (originally published in 1976) / Pitts, Carol (author)

In English and Sanskrit (romanized)

Includes bibliography

8.5" x 11" (21.59 x 27.94 cm)

Black & White on White paper

ISBN-13: 978-1478154426

ISBN-10: 147815442X

BISAC: Philosophy / Hindu

For John

Introduction to the Facsimile Edition

This book is a reproduction of my Master of Arts thesis presented to the California Institute of Asian Studies in 1976. Today that institution is known as the California Institute of Integral Studies. The original title was *The Concept of Spiritual Freedom in the Brahma Sūtras*. I have shortened the title to *Spiritual Freedom in the Brahma Sūtras* for this edition.

Much has changed since this thesis was written. At the time, computers were not readily available. The manuscript was prepared on a typewriter, and there was no way to insert diacritical marks for the Sanskrit passages. I recall marking the paper by hand, inserting each diacritic. However, it was worth the effort. Studying Indian philosophy at the Institute was a huge step for me in a long-time personal search for answers to questions such as "Who am I?", and "What is this world all about, and why?" When the time came to choose a topic for a thesis, the *Brahma Sūtras* promised to be a challenging and deep exploration of Indian traditional spiritual thought. Highly-revered in India, it is a compilation of aphorisms which gather, arrange, and justify major strands of thought in the Vedas and Upaniṣads. Within this text I chose to focus on the topic of spiritual freedom. I examined major theories and reviewed commentaries and their connections with other Indian philosophical texts. In addition, I wanted to discover if the aphorisms in the *Brahma Sutras* apply to us right now.

Since the 1980s I have been teaching classes on the Upaniṣads, the *Bhagavad Gītā*, Chi Gong, Tai Chi, and meditation. I served for over a decade as a mediator for the Alameda County Superior Court, Pleasanton, California, and currently participate in the Restorative Justice diversion program in the East Bay community.

Acknowledgments

This book was republished at the suggestion and encouragement of Les Morgan, author of *Croaking Frogs*. Many thanks, Les, for your excellent technical help and your enthusiasm for a number of projects bringing Sanskrit and Indian Philosophy to the English-speaking public.

I would also like to acknowledge Dr. Ram Karan Sharma, professor and poet, whose wisdom, kindness and far-reaching vision is an inspiration for us all.

Carol Pitts

July, 2012

Livermore, California

THE CONCEPT OF SPIRITUAL FREEDOM IN THE *BRAHMA-SŪTRA*

A Thesis

Presented to

California Institute of Asian Studies

San Francisco, California

In Partial Fulfillment

of the Requirements for the Degree

Master of Arts

by

Carol Pitts

June, 1976

CERTIFICATION OF APPROVAL

I certify that I have read "The Concept of Spiritual Freedom in the Brahma-Sutra" by Carol K. Pitts, and that in my opinion this work meets the criteria for approving a thesis submitted in partial fulfillment of requirements for the Master of Arts degree at the California Institute of Asian Studies.

Mary Oliver Tasch

Mary Oliver Tasch, Ph.D.
Professor of Psychology East and West

Hilary Anderson

Hilary Anderson, Ph.D.
Associate Professor of Integral Psychology and Self-Discipline

Rammurti S. Mishra (MD)

Rammurti S. Mishra, M.D.
Professor of Psychophysiology and Yoga Discipline

ABSTRACT

THE CONCEPT OF SPIRITUAL FREEDOM IN THE *BRAHMA-SŪTRA*

by Carol Pitts

The problem raised in this paper concerns the implications of spiritual freedom as presented in the *Brahma-Sūtra*. What have been some major philosophical theories about spiritual freedom? What value is the *Brahma-Sūtra* to modern thinkers?

To do this, the sūtras themselves are examined; commentators as Śaṅkara, Rāmānuja, and Madhva are considered, and ideas about liberation found in the Īśa and Kena Upaniṣads are compared to the sūtras. Methodology also includes historical background, definition of terms, and review of literature. To relate the tradition of the *Brahma-Sūtra* to current thinking, Dr. Rammurti S. Mishra's conception of spiritual freedom is discussed.

In conclusion it was found that while the *Brahma-Sūtra* defines spiritual freedom as oneness with Brahman, this has been interpreted in a variety of ways. It was also discovered that Dr. R. S. Mishra has made modern psychological applications to the ancient tradition of the *Brahma-Sūtra*.

ACKNOWLEDGEMENTS

It is with gratitude that I acknowledge Dr. Mary O. Tasch, Dr. Hilary Anderson and Dr. Rammurti S. Mishra, who have guided the preparation of this thesis. Also, I would like to acknowledge the late Dr. Haridas Chaudhuri who helped in the formulation of the topic. The assistance and encouragement of these individuals were greatly appreciated.

C. K. P.

TABLE OF CONTENTS

CHAPTER | Page

I. INTRODUCTION 1

I. The Problem 1
Statement of the Problem 1
Importance of the Study 1
Organization of the Remainder of the Thesis . 8

II. Historical Background 9

III. Definitions of Terms Used 16
Brahman 16
Mokṣa--Mukti 19
Māyā 21

II. REVIEW OF LITERATURE 25

I. English Translations and the Commentaries . . 25

II. Related Literature 38

III. MEANING OF SPIRITUAL FREEDOM AS FOUND IN THE BRAHMA-SŪTRA. 42

I. Content of the Brahma-Sūtra 42

II. Description of Spiritual Freedom in the Brahma-Sūtra. 51

III. Reference to Spiritual Freedom in the Īśa and Kena Upaniṣhads 58

IV. THE CONCEPT OF SPIRITUAL FREEDOM IN THE BRAHMA-SŪTRA RELATED TO A CONTEMPORARY SCHOLAR 65

CHAPTER I

INTRODUCTION

I. The Problem

Statement of the Problem

The idea of spiritual freedom has captured the imagination of philosophers and mystics for centuries. Even today some form of liberation is the main goal of a number of religious and psychological disciplines.

The problem raised in this paper concerns the meaning and implications of spiritual freedom as deliniated by a major text of Indian philosophy, the Brahma-Sūtra, with regard to (a) some major philosophical theories about spiritual freedom, (b) the commentaries on the sūtras, (c) description and pragmatic guidelines the sūtras may offer toward the realization of spiritual freedom, and (d) consideration of the value of ancient tradition of the Brahma-Sūtra to modern thought.

Importance of the Study

The questions raised are not mere philosophical speculations. The purpose for exploring them is of central importance toward coming to terms with man's age-old search for self-knowledge. It does not seem to be enough for man to take care of day to day needs, as food, jobs, homes, or even social causes. Important as they are, as soon as basic needs are met, the question of the essence of our being and purpose is confronted. As a psychiatrist Carl G. Jung commented on this fact:

> I have frequently seen people become neurotic when they content themselves with inadequate or wrong answers to the questions of life. They seek position, marriage, reputation, outward success or money, and remain unhappy and neurotic even when they have attained what they were seeking. Such people are usually confined within too narrow a spiritual horizon.[1]

The search for an understanding and experience of spiritual freedom thus has great importance to mental health and to our total evolvement.

A doubt that immediately arises is the question of the possibility or even advisability of attempting to understand a concept such as spiritual freedom. Like the concept of Brahman or God, spiritual freedom can never be adequately defined. By their very nature, definitions are analytical, fragmentary, and limiting. Ramana Maharshi has stated that the ideas of liberation and bondage are mere modifications of the mind.[2] What is needed is an intuitive,

---

[1]C.G. Jung, Memories, Dreams, Reflections (New York: Random House, 1961), p. 140.

[2]Ramana Maharshi, The Teachings of Ramana Maharshi in His Own Words, ed. Arthur Osborne (New York: Samuel Weiser, Inc., 1971), p. 120.

wholistic understanding beyond the machinations of the mind and vocabulary. The Sanskṛt mantra, "ओँ तत् सत्, Om tat sat" (Om, that inexpressible absolute reality)[3] also suggests that the reality of spiritual freedom can never be truly expressed. Why, it may be asked, bother with the attempt?

Assuming that spiritual freedom cannot be limited to a definition, it is still helpful to learn as much as possible how seers of the ages have described, experienced, and defined it. Knowledge, while not liberation itself, is a path to liberation,[4] a means by which we can become more aware of spiritual freedom and, perhaps, open the door to a higher intuition and understanding. Just as a mountain climber must start at the base of the mountain, so the seeker of spiritual freedom must begin with what is available to him.

Sri Ramakrishna has suggested how our limited knowledge produces transcendental knowledge:

> When we run a thorn in our hand we take it out by means of another thorn and throw out both. So relative knowledge alone can remove that relative ignorance which blinds the eye of the Self. But such knowledge and such ignorance are both alike included in Avidyā (ignorance); hence the

---

[3]Judith M. Tyberg, The Language of the Gods: Sanskrit Keys to India's Wisdom (Los Angeles: East-West Cultural Center, 1970), p. 21.

[4]Swami Nikhilananda, Self-Knowledge: An English Translation of Sankaracarya's Atmabodha with Notes, Comments, and Introduction (Madras: Sri Ramakrishna Math, 1967), p. 150.

> man who attains to the highest knowledge (jñāna), the knowledge of the Absolute, does away in the end with both knowledge and ignorance, being free himself from all duality.[5]

So we turn to authorities and scriptures for guidance toward a transcendental understanding. Although little known in the West, one of the most comprehensive and revered texts in Indian philosophy is the Brahma-Sūtra, also known as the Vedānta Sūtra. Radhakrishnan notes that it is held in such high esteem that anyone setting forth a new system of Indian religious and philosophic thought strives to show that his views are consistent with the Brahma-Sūtra.[6]

Written by Bādarāyaṇa about the second century B.C., the sūtras are a compilation of aphorisms which gather, arrange, and justify the major strands of thought in the Vedas and Upaniṣads.[7] The aphorisms are so succinct that they are open to a variety of interpretations. Swami Vireswarananda notes:

> . . . the Sutras . . . were intended as memory-aids to long discussions on any topic which the student had gone through with his teacher or Guru. The thought was very much condensed, for much was taken for

---

[5]Swami Vireswarananda, trans., Brahma-Sutras by Bādarāyaṇa (Calcutta: Advaita Ashrama, 1970), p. 17.

[6]S. Radhakrishnan, trans., The Brahma Sūtra: The Philosophy of Spiritual Life by Bādarāyaṇa (London: George Allen and Unwin Ltd., 1960), p. 27.

[7]S. Chatterjee and D. Datta, An Introduction to Indian Philosophy (Calcutta: University of Calcutta, 1968), p. 350.

> granted. Consequently the maximum of thought was compressed into these Sutras in as few words as possible . . . the desire for brevity was carried to such extremes that most part of the Sutra literature is now unintelligible, and this is particularly so with respect to the Vedānta-Sutras which has consequently given rise to divergent systems.[8]

The commentaries on the sūtras, written by philosophers over the centuries, become most important. Of particular note are the commentaries of Śaṅkara who lived 788-820 A.D.; Rāmānuja, about 1140 A.D.; and Madhva, about 1238 A.D.[9]

In recent years writers such as S. Radhakrishnan, Swami Vireswarananda, Swami Gambirananda, George Thibaut, S. Chatterjee, and D. Datta have offered explanations of the sūtras and their commentaries. Other philosophers as Sri Aurobindo, Haridas Chaudhuri, R.S. Mishra, and Ramana Maharshi have discussed spiritual freedom in line with the tradition of the Vedas and Upaniṣads. Although the sūtras as they stand by themselves may be difficult to understand, we have a number of sources to help render interpretation.

A brief overview of the format found in the Brahma-Sūtra may help clarify its scope and purpose. The title itself is significant.

---

[8]Vireswarananda, p. iv.

[9]S. Radhakrishnan, p. 27.

Brahman refers to God, the divine, the infinite spirit which pervades all.[10] Sūtra is from the verb "siv"--to sew. Sūtras are like pearls of thought sewn together on one string.[11]

The Brahma-Sūtra is divided into four major chapters:

1) samanvaya, समंवय --interpretations of the Upaniṣads,

2) avirodha, अविरोध --consistency of the first chapter with various sages,

3) sādhana, साधना --spiritual practice,

4) phala, फल --fruits of knowledge.[12]

Each of these chapters is divided into four parts; the parts are divided into particular topics; the topics are made up of individual sūtras. The number of sūtras included in a topic varies depending on the subject matter and need for explanation. For instance, in Chapter One, Part One, there are eleven topics, the first of which contains only one sūtra. The fifth topic in Chapter One, Part One, contains five sūtras.

Despite the varying number of sūtras, each topic has five factors:

1) viṣaya, विषय --subject matter,

2) viśaya, विशय --doubt or uncertainty,

---

[10] J. M. Tyberg, p. 4. [11] J. M. Tyberg, p. 8.

[12] Swami Gambhirananda, trans., Brahma-Sūtra Bhāṣya of Śaṅkarācārya by Śrī Śaṅkarācārya (Calcutta: Advaita Ashrama, 1972), pp. xiv-xxi.

3) pūrva-pakṣa, पूर्वपक्ष --prima facie view or statement of an objection,

4) siddhānta, सिद्धान्त --established conclusion,

5) saṁgati, संगति --connection between the different sections.[13]

Thus it can be seen that the Brahma-Sūtra attempts to look at the issues it raises from every viewpoint, comparing and contrasting possibilities and coming to specific conclusions. As an aid in determining the outlines of various views of spiritual freedom, it is invaluable. But that is not all. According to Swami Vireswarananda,[14] the Brahma-Sūtra, as the Upaniṣads, contains a variety of doctrines meant for people at different stages of development. Not all people comprehend truth in the same manner. For instance, a beginner is taught to worship God, perform rituals and spiritual practices. Later, the divine Brahman is declared to be one with the human soul. As the Sanskṛt mantra puts it, "तत् त्वं असि, tat tvam asi,"--Thou art that.[15] The variety of approaches offers fulfillment of an individual's need, wherever he happens to be in his inquiry.

The comprehensiveness, the systematic approach, the offering of support and objections to particular topics all contribute to making

---

[13]S. Radhakrishnan, p. 24. [14]Vireswarananda, p. liv.

[15]J. M. Tyberg, p. 19.

the Brahma-Sūtra an especially important text on the subject of spiritual freedom.

Organization of the Remainder of the Thesis

An analysis of the concept of spiritual freedom as found in the Brahma-Sūtra will form the greater part of this thesis. Discussion will also include: historical background, definition of some key concepts and Sanskṛt terms relevant to the idea of spiritual freedom; review of commentators of the Brahma-Sūtra; discussion of related literature; comparison of the idea of spiritual freedom found in the Brahma-Sūtra to that found in the Īśa and Kena Upaniṣads, as well as a summary and conclusion.

In addition there will be a chapter on the application of these ideas to those found in a modern philosopher and scientist, Dr. Rammurti S. Mishra. Theories written many centuries ago must be tested to see how they fit into the context of modern thinking. As Radhakrishnan states:

> The truth which claims to be universal requires to be continually re-created. It cannot be something already possessed that only needs to be re-transmitted. In every generation, it has to be renewed. Otherwise it tends to become dogma which soothes us and induces complacency but does not encourage the supreme personal adventure. Tradition should be a principle not of conservatism but of growth and regeneration . . . By the free use of reason and experience we appropriate truth and keep tradition in a continuous process of evolution. If it is to have a hold on people's minds, it must reckon

> with the vast reorientation of thought that has taken place. By reinterpreting the past afresh, each generation stamps it with something of its own problems and preoccupations.[16]

One modern scholar was chosen to see how the tradition of the Brahma-Sūtra is being expressed today. The work of Dr. Rammurti S. Mishra is a particularly valuable bridge for the gap between the old and the new. As a samnyāsin monk in Advaita Vedānta and as a Sanskṛt scholar, he has studied the sūtras and the Upaniṣads. Also a medical doctor with specialties in endocrinology, neuro-surgery, and psychiatry, he brings to his analysis of spiritual freedom an understanding of modern scientific discipline. It is hoped that this discussion will indicate the relevance and implications of the Brahma-Sūtra for today.

II. Historical Background

Before the study of spiritual freedom and the Brahma-Sūtra is begun, a general overview of Indian philosophical tradition and historic background needs to be considered.

The early Indo-Aryans, living on the banks of the Ganges River in prehistoric times, questioned the meaning of life, death, and suffering. They wondered if there was an ultimate reality, a

---

[16] S. Radhakrishnan, p. 8.

first cause underlying man and the universe.[17] They used reasoning, self-discipline, and meditation to study these age-old problems. The scriptures which emerged from this period are called the Vedas, from the Sanskṛt root "vid" meaning "to know." Tyberg defines the Vedas as "collections of illuminating hymns to the gods and goddesses of inner and outer nature."[18] The Hindus believe that the Vedas are eternal and "not inspired but expired by God;"[19] thus they are śruti, from "śru" meaning "to hear," or that which is heard directly from infinite intelligence.

There are four main Vedas, each having a definite focus: 1) the Rig-Veda, ऋग्वेद, containing verses addressed to devas or Gods, symbolic of the higher powers in man;[20] 2) the Yajur-Veda, यजुर्वेद, concerning right action, sacrificial rites symbolic of man's attaining divinity; 3) Sāma-Veda, सामवेद, or joyful chants; 4) Atharva Veda, अथर्ववेद, formulas to counteract evil and disease.

Nearly all of the Vedas each have four sections: the Saṁhita or religion of nature, of poets;[21] Brāhmaṇas, the exegesis and religion of law and of priests; Āraṇyaka, the interpretation of sacrifice;

---

[17]S. Nikhilananda, p. 5. [18]J.M. Tyberg, p. 5.

[19]S. Vireswarananda, p. i. [20]J.M. Tyberg, p. 87.

[21]Chandradhar Sharma, A Critical Survey of Indian Philosophy (Delhi: Motilal Banarsidass, 1964), pp. 14-15.

and the Upaniṣads or spiritual philosophy. These sections related to the various stages of life that a Hindu was expected to experience. At first were his student years as a brahma-cārin when he prepared himself for life and read all the Vedas, but expecially the Saṁhita; then came his years as a householder, or gṛhastha, when he raised a family and served his community, and when he followed the teaching of Brāhmaṇas; the forest-dweller or vānaprasthi was the stage where the individual still had a family but gradually gave up his civic and social duties to spend more time in study and meditation, particularly giving attention to the Āraṇyaka; and lastly, those who gave up the world totally in search of truth and freedom were called samnyāsin and studied the Upaniṣads.[22]

The Vedas are the foundation of Hinduism, often called Sanātana Dharma (the eternal religion), because of its basis on eternal principles. Hinduism is also called Vaiḍka Dharma, because it is based on the teachings of the Vedas.[23]

Still another type of division is made in the Vedas. They may be divided roughly into two parts: the Karmakāṇḍa, dealing with rituals and sacrifices, and Jñānakāṇḍa, which teaches philosophic wisdom. This division describes the two main thrusts of the Vedas,

---

[22]S. Nikhilananda, pp. 22-26. [23]Ibid., p. 8.

how to deal with worldly matters as well as realization of highest good.[24]

Included in the Jñānakāṇḍa are the Upaniṣads, also known as Vedānta as they are the concluding chapters (anta) of the Vedas. Vedānta as we know it now, however, was systematized and developed in later years by such writers as Bādarāyaṇa, Śaṅkara, and others.

The Upaniṣads (from the verb "sad"--"to sit," plus the prefixes "upa"--"near," and "ni"--"down," hence implying "to sit down near" the teacher)[25] teaches knowledge of Brahman. One hundred eight Upaniṣads are known, twelve of which are called major Upaniṣads. They are: Aitareya, Taittirīya, Chāndogya, Bṛhadāraṇyaka, Muṇḍaka, Māṇḍūkya, Īśa, Kena, Kaṭha, Praśna, Śvetāśvatara, and Kaivalya.

According to Swami Nikhilananda,

> The Upaniṣads cannot be called a formal and systematic philosophy in the usual sense of the term. The Hindus look upon them as containing revelations of supersensuous truths regarding the soul, the universe, and Ultimate Reality. The Vedas are called Śruti (hearing), because they were taught by word of mouth. Outwardly the Upaniṣads contain contradictory statements, and so the texts were for a long time exhaustively discussed in order that the precise ideas of the ṛṣis might be ascertained. Vyāsa[26] composed a treatise known as the Vedānta-Sūtras

---

[24] S. Nikhilananda, p. 10. [25] J.M. Tyberg, p. 5.

[26] S. Radhakrishnan, p. 22, notes that Bādarāyaṇa "is sometimes said to be Vyāsa, literally the arranger. He is said to have arranged the Vedas in their present form."

> or Brahma-Sūtras, in which he reconciled the many apparent contradictions. This work is now regarded as a standard treatise on Vedānta philosophy, the first successful attempt to systematize the views of the Upaniṣads . . .[27]

Poetry is used extensively in the Upaniṣads as there are limitations in ordinary language when the intent is to express the mystery of truth. As Sharma states:

> These poetic-philosophic works are full of grand imagery, extremely charming and lucid expression abounding in crystal clarity (prasāda guṇa). To the mind, they bring sound philosophical doctrines and to the heart, peace and freedom. They are full of Ānanda or Supreme Joy out of which all things arise, by which they live, and into which they return again.[28]

Also, Radhakrishnan mentions that the Upaniṣads use the language of meditation, samādhi-bhāṣā, as "the most appropriate response to the spiritual experience is silence or poetry."[29]

The "visions of truth," which the Upaniṣads describe, are called "darśana," from the root "dṛś"--meaning "to see."[30] The purpose of these writings was to enable the student to see truth directly. The various schools which developed out of the Upaniṣads are also called darśana.

---

[27]S. Nikhilananda, p. 15. [28]C. Sharma, p. 18.

[29]S. Radhakrishnan, p. 20. [30]Ibid.

The vast influence of the Upaniṣads is realized when one looks at the number of later schools of philosophy or darśana which take fundamental ideas from these early texts. Indian philosophy in its entirety may be divided into two groups: the āstika, based on the Vedas, and nāstika, not accepting the authority of the Vedas. Patañjali describes the āstika as believing in a world beyond the present and the nāstika as denying its existence; Manu states that anyone "who repudiates Vedic doctrines is a nāstika."[31]

Six darśana are included in āstika: Nyāya, Vaiśeṣika, Sāṅkhya, Yoga, Mīmāṁsā, and Vedānta; nāstika includes Cārvaka, Jaina, and four schools of Baudha.[32]

Even the nāstika groups have used the concepts found in the Upaniṣads. Sharma points out:

> The heterodox Jainism has taken its idealism and its doctrine of Karma from the Upaniṣads. The heterodox Buddhism derives its idealism, monism, absolutism, the theory of momentariness of all worldly things, the theory of Karma, the distinction between the empirical and the absolute standpoints, and the theory that Ignorance is the root-cause of this cycle of birth-and-death and that Nirvāṇa can be attained by right knowledge alone, from the Upaniṣads.[33]

Both the āstika and nāstika have as a basic purpose release

---

[31]S. Radhakrishnan, p. 20. [32]J.M. Tyberg, p. 217.

[33]C. Sharma, p. 31.

from the bondage to time. (A possible exception is the Cārvakas, who state that only matter which is perceived in the here and now has any reality.)[34] Beliefs as to the nature of this release vary from dissolution to life in God. But they agree that ignorance, spiritual blindness causes bondage and that knowledge leads to release.[35]

Of particular importance to this study of spiritual freedom in the Brahma-Sūtra are the Sāṅkhya and Vedānta darśanas. Briefly, Sāṅkhya is commonly interpreted to be dualistic realism. Two ultimate realities are postulated: nature and consciousness. In the Vedānta system, one ultimate reality is accepted. The Brahma-Sūtra supports the Vedāntic position. Various interpretations of the nature of this one ultimate reality are debated in the Brahma-Sūtra and will be considered in this paper. Some of the differences are subtle, yet lead to far-reaching variations in approach to the concept of spiritual freedom.

The Brahma-Sūtra, as mentioned earlier, is an aphoristic summary of the Upaniṣads and attempts to justify, systematize, and reconcile its various strands of thought. Hence this summary covers a vast area, both in philosophic scope and in terms of the time span of centuries.

---

[34]S. Chatterjee and D. Datta, pp. 25-6.

[35]S. Radhakrishnan, p. 21.

III. Definitions of Terms Used

Having taken an overview of the historical background out of which the Brahma-Sūtra emerged, we can now explore a few terms which are particularly relevant to the concept of spiritual freedom.

Brahman ब्रह्मन्

At the core of Hindu philosophy is the concept of Brahman. It is the underlying principle of all, the divine, God, the absolute, infinite spirit.[36] The root "bṛh" means "to expand." Monier-Williams gives expansion, evolution, swelling of spirit or soul, the universal divine essence as part of his definition.[37]

The first statement made in the Brahma-Sūtra is "athāto brahma-jijñāsā," meaning, "Now therefore the desire to know Brahman;"[38] another translation reads, "Hence (is to be undertaken) thereafter a deliberation on Brahman;"[39] or "Now: therefore the inquiry (into the real nature) of Brahman."[40] So the study of the nature of Brahman is the first and most basic inquiry.

---

[36] J.M. Tyberg, p. 4.

[37] Monier Monier-Williams, A Sanskrit-English Dictionary (Oxford: Clarendon Press, 1970), pp. 737-8.

[38] S. Radhakrishnan, p. 227. [39] S. Gambhirananda, p. 6.

[40] S. Vireswarananda, p. 19.

The Chāndogya Upaniṣad describes Brahman: "Verily, this whole world is Brahman, from which he comes forth, without which he will be dissolved, and in which he breathes. Tranquil, one should meditate on it."[41] Brahman, the supreme reality, transcends all, yet it underlies all as their background. Nothing is lost. Sharma refers to the story of Bhṛgu in the Taittirīya Upaniṣad when he writes: "Matter is not lost in life; life is not lost in mind; mind is not lost in reason; reason is not lost in bliss. Brahman pervades them all."[42]

Haridas Chaudhuri gives a definition of Brahman:

> The term "Brahman" etymologically means the Great, the Supreme. It sums up the Hindu view of the nature of ultimate reality. "Brahman" is the cosmic principle of existence, the ultimate unifying and integrating principle of the universe. It has two inseparable aspects or modes of existence: "nirguṇa" and "saguṇa," impersonal and personal, indeterminable and self-determining. "Brahman," which is at once indeterminable and self-determining, is thus the unity of freedom and creativity, time and eternity, ineffable silence and perpetual self-expression.[43]

This description of Brahman as all inclusive, both having qualities (saguṇa) and not having qualities (nirguṇa), is found also in the Māṇḍūkya Upaniṣad. In this Upaniṣad, a detailed analysis of

---

[41] Chāndogya Upaniṣad, III. 14.1.

[42] C. Sharma, p. 25.

[43] Haridas Chaudhuri, "The Concept of Brahman in Hindu Philosophy," Philosophy East and West, IV (April 1954), pp. 47-48.

aum ॐ , the verbal symbol of Brahman,[44] is given. "A" refers to the waking state, to activity. "U" is cognition of internal objects, the dream state. "M" is the state of deep sleep where consciousness enjoys peace, all impressions become one. "The fourth is that which has no elements, which cannot be spoken of, into which the world is resolved, benign, non-dual. Thus the syllable aum is the very self. He who known it thus enters the self with his self."[45] So Brahman, here represented by the sound aum, contains both the unmanifested absolute and manifestation.

Although all is Brahman, some other terms are used to specify particular aspects of the divine. Brahman refers to the infinite divine; Īśvara ईश्वर to the universal divine. The function of Īśvara is further delineated: Brahmā ब्रह्मा as creator, Viṣṇu विष्णु as preserver, and Śiva शिव as destroyer and regenerator.[46]

Jīva जीव is the life-spark in all living things; in man it is the individual self. It is Brahman or pure consciousness associated with individual ignorance.

> So when the pure Ātman is superimposed on the attributes of the mind, the senses and the body, he gets the name Jīva -- the doer of deeds and the enjoyer of their fruits. It is this false shadow of Ātman, the Jīva, that undergoes

---

[44] S. Radhakrishnan, *The Principle Upaniṣads*, (London: George Allen & Unwin Ltd., 1969), pp. 695-98.

[45] Ibid., p. 701. [46] J. M. Tyberg, p. 4.

all troubles of life, such as birth and death.[47]

Ātman, आत्मन् according to Mishra, is the term used for the "divine soul lying dormant in all living beings but able to be manifested to its fullest in man by the practice of meditation. It is variously called Self, Universal Principle, Supreme Consciousness."[48]

Although some philosophic schools make distinctions which will be noted later, Brahman and Ātman are often used synonymously. They are the same reality seen from two sides: the subjective side is Ātman, and the objective is Brahman. The absolute is both subject and object and transcends them both.[49] The mantras "I am Brahman" and "Ātman is Brahman" express this.

Mokṣa--Mukti मोक्ष मुक्ति

Mokṣa and mukti mean liberation or spiritual freedom. Civil and political freedoms or human rights that can be legislated, as freedom of speech, are not under discussion here. Instead, mokṣa implies an experiential realization of reality. On a practical level, it affects the individual's attitude toward all that occurs in life as

---

[47] Swami Sarvananda, Kaṭhopaniṣad (Madras: Sri Ramakrishna Math, 1968), p. 62.

[48] Rammurti S. Mishra, Fundamentals of Yoga (New York: The Julian Press, 1959), p. 242.

[49] C. Sharma, p. 25.

he realizes his true relationship or oneness with Brahman and the world. In the words of Radhakrishnan, mokṣa is "release, emancipation, union with the Ultimate."[50] Vedānta suggests it is achieved by the realization that the individual and the absolute are non-dual. What exactly is meant by union with Brahman differs with various philosophers. These will be considered in a later section of this paper.

Apavarga अपवर्ग is a related word meaning completion, release, liberation and freedom of the soul from transmigration.[51]

Līlā लीला means cosmic play of the divine.[52] It implies the divine being "creating and re-creating Himself in Himself for the sheer bliss of that self-creation, of the self-representation--Himself the play, Himself the player, Himself the playground."[53] Haridas Chaudhuri comments that līlā is cosmic non-attached love. He suggests that there are two basic ways to perceive the non-temporal divine: 1) the void, abstract transcendence, mystic denial; 2) on a deeper level, the denial itself is denied in a higher affirmation.

> It is realized that if the world is nothing apart from God, God is nothing apart from the world. . . (such an understanding is) the basis of love as selfless participation in the creative advance of cosmic evolution. In Hindu

---

[50] S. Radhakrishnan, The Brahma-Sūtra, p. 570.

[51] Ibid., p. 567.

[52] J. M. Tyberg, p. 158.

[53] Sri Aurobindo, The Life Divine, II (Pondicherry: Sri Aurobindo Ashram), Glossary, p. 19.

philosophy such participation has been called līlā, i.e., joyful cooperation with the dynamic world spirit.[54]

Turīya तुरीय and samādhi समाधि are terms also associated with mokṣa. They refer to that state of consciousness which is totally aware of being one with Brahman.

Māyā माया

Māyā has a two-fold aspect. It is the creative force in the cosmos; the root "mā" means to give form, to measure, to limit.[55] Also, māyā is illusion, formed from a limited view or ignorance. The example is often given of mistaking a rope for a snake in a darkened room. The illusion not only conceals from view the real nature of the rope, but also makes it appear as something else.[56] So it is with māyā. The creating aspect of God gives form to matter; this form conceals its real nature and makes it appear as other than God.

In its illusion producing aspect, māyā is also called avidyā अविद्या or ajñāna अज्ञान , that is, wrong knowledge, ignorance, nescience.

---

[54]Haridas Chaudhuri, Integral Yoga: The Concept of Harmonious and Creative Living (San Francisco: California Institute of Asian Studies), pp. 97-8.

[55]J.M. Tyberg, p. 36. [56]S. Chatterjee and D. Datta, p. 370.

Chatterjee and Datta point out that for God, māyā is only the will to create appearance and this appearance does not deceive God. But most of us are deceived and see many objects here instead of one Brahman or God. For us, māyā is an illusion producing ignorance.[57]

Prakṛti प्रकृति is defined as supreme nature; puruṣa पुरुष as supreme consciousness. The distinction is, according to Sri Aurobindo:

> . . . the fundamental division of the Purusha, the conscious soul who knows and sees and by his vision creates and ordains, and the Prakriti, the Force Soul or Nature--Soul which is his knowledge and his vision, his creation and his all-ordaining power.[58]

In the Śvetāśvataropaniṣad, "prakṛti is māyā."[59] Here, prakṛti is a power of God and is completely dependent on God. This is not to be confused with the prakṛti of the Sāṅkhya philosophic school. In Sāṅkhya, prakṛti is also supreme nature, but is a separate and independent function from puruṣa, existing entirely on its own. The Brahma-Sūtra takes the position found in the Śvetāśvataropaniṣad. Prakṛti is the subtle cause of the universe, the Brahma-Sūtra comments, but at the same time it is totally dependent on God. "On account of its dependence (on the Lord), it

---

[57] S. Chatterjee and D. Datta, p. 371.

[58] S. Aurobindo, pp. 24-25.

[59] S. Radhakrishnan, The Principal Upaniṣads, p. 734.

fits in (with our theory)."[60] Nescience cannot create of itself without the instrumentality of Brahman.

Māyā or prakṛti, in the sense of being dependent on Brahman, consists of three guṇas or qualities.

> The three guṇas are the ingredients of māyā; they may be compared to three strands which constitute the rope of māyā, the rope by which māyā binds man to the illusory world. Māyā has no existence independent of the guṇas. The three guṇas are present, in varying degrees, in all objects, gross or subtle, including the mind, the buddhi, and the ego. The food which nourishes our body, the thought which is the function of the mind, the duty which elevates a man from the animal level, charity, worship, sacrifice--in short, everything belonging to the universe of māyā--contains these three guṇas.[61]

When all the guṇas are at equilibrium, there is non-manifestation or cosmic rest. If the equilibrium is disturbed, at the will of Brahman, the universe begins to manifest itself. The three guṇas always exist together, in varying proportions. Rajas, रजस् from the root "raj"--"to grow," is the guṇa of activity and energy; tamas, तमस् from the root "tam"--"to perish, to grow sad," is inertia and has a veiling power. Its influence on man is ignorance and lassitude.

> After tamas has veiled the true nature of the Self, rajas exerts its projecting-power and creates the many fantasies

---

[60] S. Vireswarananda, p. 121.

[61] S. Nikhilananda, p. 65.

> that constitute an unenlightened man's practical life. And alas, even scholars well versed in philosophy cannot escape its hypnotic spell. It is the mother of delusion.[62]

Sattva, सत्त्व from "sat"--"being," is the balancing guṇa in nature and manifests itself as purity, harmony, and virtue. Although sattva can lead one toward mokṣa, it is nevertheless still a part of the veiling power of māyā. Sattva can bind one to happiness.

Swami Nikhilananda relates a story to demonstrate the functions of the three guṇas.[63] Three robbers attack a man in the forest. The first, tamas, tries to kill him; the second, rajas, convinces tamas not to kill, but ties the man to a tree and takes his treasures. The last, sattva, releases him and takes him to the edge of the forest, setting him on the path to freedom.

---

[62] S. Nilhilananda, pp. 66-7. [63] Ibid., p. 68.

CHAPTER II

REVIEW OF LITERATURE

I. English Translations and the Commentaries

Four English translations of the Brahma-Sūtra are available: the French Indologist George Thibaut, whose Part I appeared in 1890 and Part II in 1896; two monks of the Ramakrishna Order offer translations, Swami Vireswarananda, 1936, and Swami Gambhirananda, 1965; and Sarvepalli Radhakrishnan's translation, extensive notes and background material was published in 1960. Each translation includes, in varying amounts, some of the traditional commentaries. As mentioned previously, the commentaries assume a good deal of importance as the sūtras themselves are a shorthand to remind the student of long discussions with the teacher.

The earliest extant commentator is Śaṅkara, who lived in the late 8th and early 9th Century A.D. It is believed that there were commentaries preceeding Śaṅkara, as Bodhāyana, but their works have been lost and are unavailable.[1] Other commentaries which have

---

[1]S. Radhakrishnan, The Brahma-Sūtra: The Philosophy of Spiritual Life (London: Geroge Allen & Unwin Ltd., 1960), p. 27.

come down to us and will be considered are Rāmānuja, about 1140 A.D.; Madhva, 1238; Nimbārka, 1150; Vallabha, 1540; and Baladeva, 1725.

All of these commentaries expound doctrines found in the Upaniṣads and referred to in the Brahma-Sūtra.[2] Instead of raising new issues, they follow one or the other of the ancient traditions. For instance, in the text of the Brahma-Sūtra, references are made to Jaimini, Āśmarathya, and Bādari in I. 2. 28, 29, and 30 respectively. It is to the credit of the Brahma-Sūtra that while systematizing the ideas of the Upaniṣads, it covers a variety of interpretations and traditions.

Perhaps the foremost commentator is Śaṅkara. Each of the English translations base their notes primarily on his writings. Both Thibaut and Swami Gambhirananda mention Śaṅkara in the title of their books. Swami Vireswarananda, as a monk of the Ramakrishna Order espousing advaita philosophy of non-dualism, favors the tradition of Śaṅkara. Radhakrishnan offers a more detailed analysis of all the commentators and traditions. However, in the arrangement of the sūtras, which can lead to variations in interpretations, he uses Śaṅkara's format:

---

[2] Radhakrishnan, p. 26.

> There are slight variations in the readings of the sūtras in Brahma-Sūtra. Sometimes one sūtra is read as two or two as one. Sometimes the last word of a sūtra is added to the beginning of the next one. These variations lead to divergent interpretations. . . . We have adopted Ś(aṅkara)'s reading as the standard and noted the divergences from it. His numbering of the sūtras is adopted.[3]

Also, Radhakrishnan states in his preface: "In this book I have followed principally Śaṅkara's commentary which is accepted generally by others except in those places where doctrinal differences are indicated."[4]

Although Thibaut was writing years before the other translators, he was well aware of the impact of Śaṅkara on Indian philosophy. In a lengthy introduction, he writes:

> But on the modern investigator, who can neither consider himself bound by the authority of a name however great, nor is likely to look to any Indian system of thought for the satisfaction of his speculative wants, it is clearly incumbent not to acquiesce from the out-set in the interpretations given of the Vedānta-sūtras--and the Upanishads--by Śaṅkara and his school, but to submit them ,as far as that can be done, to a critical investigation.
>
> This is a task which would have to be undertaken even if Śaṅkara's view as to the true meaning of the Sūtras and Upanishads had never been called into doubt on Indian soil, although in that case it could perhaps hardly be entered upon with much hope of success; but it becomes much more urgent, and at the same time more feasible, when we meet

---

[3] S. Radhakrishnan, pp. 24-5. [4] Ibid., p. 11.

> in India itself with systems claiming to be Vedāntic and based on interpretations of the Sūtras and Upanishads more or less differing from those of Śaṅkara.[5]

Thibaut picks Rāmānuja as one of the foremost commentators representing a divergent point of view. He points out that not only does there seem to be a logical basis for Rāmānuja's interpretation, but he follows the ancient Vedāntic tradition of Bodhāyana and is close to Bhāgavatas or Pañcarātras.[6]

After giving a detailed analysis of points of difference between Śaṅkara and Rāmānuja, some of which we will cover later, Thibaut comes to a two-fold conclusion. While Rāmānuja may be closer in the literal sense to the Brahma-Sūtra, Śaṅkara's fundamental doctrines are "in greater harmony with the essential teachings of the Upaniṣads than those of other Vedāntic systems."[7] Śaṅkara has allowed for clearly existing differences in a way which other systems attempt to obliterate. This raises another question which Thibaut discusses but leaves open: Does, then, Śaṅkara more faithfully represent Upaniṣadic tradition as a whole than does Bādarāyaṇa's Brahma-Sūtra? Thibaut hints that the period in which Bādarāyaṇa wrote may well have attempted to popularize their philosophy by

---

[5] George Thibaut, trans., The Vedanta Sutras of Bādarāyaṇa: With the Commentary by Śaṅkara, I (New York: Dover Publications, 1962), pp. xv-xvi.

[6] Ibid., p. xxii. [7] Ibid., p. cxxiv.

referring more heavily to the personal aspect of God rather than the non-dualistic stance found in the Upaniṣads and, much later, in Śaṅkara.[8]

Although not mentioning Thibaut, Swami Vireswarananda in his introduction seems to be speaking directly to the questions raised above.

> There is a strong opinion current amongst scholars today that whatever be the merit of Sankara's metaphysical doctrines considered by themselves or even as doctrines elucidating the teachings of the Upanishads, he is not faithful to Bādarāyana in his interpretation of the Sutras. . . . In short, their view is that the system of Bādarāyana is a theistic system which has more affinities with the systems of Rāmānuja and Nimbārka than with Sankara's pure Non-dualism.[9]

After listing the reasons he feels Śaṅkara is faithful to the Brahma-Sūtras as well as the Upaniṣads, Swami Vireswarananada concludes:

> . . . we do not mean to suggest that Sankara's interpretation of the Sutras is the only true one. Rather our object has been to show that Sankara, too, like the other great commentators, is justified in interpreting the Sutras in the way he has done. . . . The fact is, Bādarāyana has systematized the philosophy of the Upanishads in his work, and like them his Sutras are also all-comprehensive. The Upanishads . . . contain various doctrines which are meant for people at different stages of spiritual evolution. They are not contradictory, but rather they are based on

---

[8]G. Thibaut, pp. cxxvi-viii.

[9]Swami Vireswarananda, Brahma-Sutras: With Text, Word-for-Word Translation, English Rendering, Comments and Index (Calcutta: Advaita Ashrama, 1970), p. xiv.

> the principle of Adhikāribheda, as all are not capable of apprehending the same truth . . . Nearly every chapter in the Upanishads begins with dualistic teaching or upāsanā and ends with a grand flourish of Advaita . . . From this point of view we are inclined to think that of all the commentators Sankara has done the greatest justice to the Sutrakāra . . .[10]

Regardless of how closely one decides Śaṅkara followed the Brahma-Sūtra, his commentary seems to be unquestionably important and an intrinsic part of an analysis of the sūtras. We will now turn to a discussion of the main points of his philosophy and compare these to the other major commentators. Each commentator, it will be recalled, represents an ancient, traditional line of thought based on the Upaniṣads.

Śaṅkara's school of philosophy is called Advaita, unqualified non-dualism, and is said to follow the varāha-sahodara-vṛtti tradition.[11] The most basic tenet of this tradition is that Brahman and the world are one. In fact, the word "one" is limiting in that it might suggest a previous duality that has become one. Brahman and the individual manifestation are totally and eternally non-dual, non-different.

Absolute or nirguṇa Brahman is devoid of any attributes or form.[12] Some places in the Upaniṣads Brahman is given attributes,

---

[10] S. Vireswarananda, pp. liv-lv.

[11] S. Radhakrishnan, p. 26. [12] Ibid., p. 452.

but this is just for meditational purposes. Brahman is non-dual, pure consciousness. It appears as many, as the sun reflects differently in vessels holding water.[13]

The question is raised: How do we account for the variety of manifestations in the world, the appearance of many individuals? A unique aspect of Śaṅkara's viewpoint is his development of the concept of māyā. As was mentioned in Chapter I, māyā has a two-fold aspect: it is the creating aspect of God which gives form to matter and this form conceals God's real nature, making it appear as many. Śaṅkara claims that the world is not real and not unreal. As Radhakrishnan puts it:

> Ś(aṅkara) suggests that the world is an appearance due to ignorance and so this appearance does not affect the cause in any way, even as a magician is not affected by the illusion he creates for others . . . We cannot say that an illusion is non-existent. Something is perceived though it is interpreted wrongly. The rope which is perceived as a snake is contradicted when the perception of snake disappears. But the world does not disappear. When the appearance of the world is said to be anirvacanīya, all that is meant is that it is unique . . . The world is sat because it exists for a time; is it asat for it does not exist for all time . . . The world is unreal when viewed apart from its basis in the ultimate reality or Brahman. When viewed in its relation to Brahman, we find that all this is Brahman: sarvam khalv idaṁ brahma.[14]

---

[13] S. Radhakrishnan, p. 455.

[14] Ibid., pp. 33-34.

Only because of ignorance does the individual soul seem different from Brahman, and when the ignorance is removed the soul realizes its non-duality with nirguṇa Brahman. This is mokṣa, release, spiritual freedom.[15]

According to Thibaut, the two-fold reality, sat and asat, of the world is a unique development of Śaṅkara. It is not, however, an addition to the system found in the Upaniṣads, "but only a development from within, no graft but only growth."[16]

Śaṅkara's concept of māyā has often been misunderstood. It is easy and misleading to quote Śaṅkara as stating the world is illusion and therefore unreal. Yet he made a definite effort to make his point clear.

His introduction to the Brahma-Sūtra discusses adhyāsa (to sit down, occupy one's seat, cohabit[17]) or superimposition. "Superimposition is the cognition as something of what is not that."[18] The example is given of mistaking a rope for a snake. The rope's reality is unchanged but, due to ignorance, the observer superimposes a false identity on the rope and reacts with fear. In the translation of

---

[15] S. Gambhirananda, p. x. [16] G. Thibaut, p. cxxv.

[17] Monier Monier-Williams, A Sanskrit-English Dictionary (Oxford: Clarendon Press, 1970), p. 23.

[18] S. Radhakrishnan, p. 232.

Swami Gambhirananda, adhyāsa is "an awareness, similar in nature to memory, that arises on a different (foreign) basis as a result of some past experience . . . it consists in the superimposition of the attributes of one thing on another."[19] Owing to an absence of discrimination, man has a tendency to say, "This is mine," or "I am healthy," thus mixing up reality and unreality as a result of superimposing the things themselves or their attributes on each other. Discrimination between self and not-self is essential for mokṣa. Superimposition is ignorance; determination of the nature of reality is knowledge.[20]

> Our experience is based on an identification of the Self with the body, the senses, etc. This is the beginningless māyā. In our waking life we identify the Self with many unreal things . . . Ś(aṅkara) argues that the Self is of the nature of pure consciousness and it is permanent and not momentary.[21]

Only by right knowledge is final release experienced. Prayer and worship can lead to brahma-loka and the realization of the nature of saguṇa without total identification with nirguṇa Brahman. When true knowledge dawns, it at once removes all ignorance and bondage. True knowledge cannot be produced by injunctions or prohibitions; it is not a mental activity but is an existent fact.[22] Prayer may help

---

[19]S. Gambhirananda, p. 2. [20]S. Radhakrishnan, p. 232.

[21]Ibid., p. 31.

[22]Chandradhar Sharma, A Critical Survey of Indian Philosophy (Delhi: Motilal Banarsidass, 1964), p. 287.

purify the mind to help us receive true knowledge which alone can enable us to become one with the absolute.

Rāmānuja's philosophy has a different emphasis. He attempts a combination of absolutism with a personal theism. His system is called Viśiṣṭādvaita or non-dualism qualified by difference, based on the Puruṣa-sūkta of the Ṛgveda and the Pañcarātra[23] as well as the Bodhāyana-vṛtti.[24] There is one God but Rāmānuja does not make a distinction between nirguṇa Brahman and saguṇa Brahman. God is saguṇa, with qualities. The world and Brahman are equally real and are non-separate; they are different from each other yet are connected. As the head of a cow is not the whole cow, so man is one inseparable part of God but can never be the entirety.

Since saguṇa Brahman includes the world and everything in it, all knowledge is true. Rāmānuja refutes Śaṅkara's doctrine of māyā as producing illusion of any sort. The snake and the rope are made of the same elements so no unreal object is perceived.

Liberation is not a merging with God but an intuitive awareness by the soul of its own nature as a part of the supreme. Individuality is retained and the soul partakes of some of the qualities of Īśvara or saguṇa Brahman. Devotion and self-surrender leads to mokṣa;

---

[23]Ibid., p. 336.

[24]S. Radhakrishnan, p. 26.

self-surrender is possible when karmas are fulfilled, when there is knowledge of the scriptures and when divine grace changes constant thoughts on God to an immediate intuition. Mokṣa is also freedom from avidyā.

Radhakrishnan[25] notes that Śaṅkara and Rāmānuja represent two uninterrupted traditions in Indian philosophy which, despite their apparent discrepancies and scholastic arguments, are complementary to each other. For instance, while Śaṅkara is a non-dualist, he had great faith in devotion to a personal God, as his hymns attest.

Madhva interpreted the Brahma-Sūtra as proporting dualism. His philosophy, Dvaita, also has its roots in ancient tradition, Haya-grīva-brahma-vidyā.

He believes that saguṇa Brahman and the world are eternally separate. The world, experience, and bondage are all equally real and not māyā. A personal God caused the universe; since none of us feel omniscient or omnipotent, which are divine qualities, we must be different from God.

Mokṣa means coming close to God, not a state on non-duality with the absolute. The soul is intelligence, veiled by avidyā. The path to liberation includes devotion, good works, experience, knowledge.

---

[25] S. Radhakrishnan, p. 51.

There are three kinds of people: those who attain salvation; those who pass through cycles of birth and re-birth; and those damned in hell eternally. Four kinds of salvation or liberation are listed: entrance of freed souls into God's body; sight of God; nearness to God; and an attendant to God.[26]

The last three commentators to be considered express variations to the above philosophers. Although they will not be referred to later in this discussion, it is well to note a few major points which they raise.

Nimbārka's Dvaitādvaita or Dualistic Non-Dualism, owes much to Rāmānuja. Nimbārka believes in one reality with three aspects: God, soul, and matter. The ruler of the universe is God in the form of Kṛṣṇa. Both Rāmānuja and Nimbārka suggest that the world is real like Brahman and that it is both different and non-different from the supreme. For Rāmānuja, the difference from God cannot be separate from identity with God; but with Nimbārka, both identity and difference are equally real. Matter and souls are not attributes of God, as Rāmānuja states, for then God would have imperfections and would change. Instead, matter and souls are "powers" of God.[27] With Nimbārka there is a subtle emphasis on the world's difference from God.

---

[26] S. Radhakrishnan, p. 65. [27] C. Sharma, p. 377.

The difference between souls and God remains even in liberation. Mokṣa is the full development of one's own nature. Devotion and God's grace are the factors which open the individual to true knowledge and, hence, to liberation.

Vallabha's Śuddhādvaita (Pure Non-Dualism) teaches that the individual soul is of the same substance as Brahman. Vallabha, although similar in many respects to the non-dualism of Śaṅkara, rejects the doctrine of māyā as impure. Brahman, who is being-awareness-bliss (sat-chid-ānanda), manifests himself as the universe without undergoing any change. In the material world, only the existence aspect of God is perceptible; while knowledge and bliss are obscured. In the individual soul, bliss is unrealized, but existence and knowledge are manifested.[28]

Bhakti, as love and service to God, alone is the means to salvation. No individual effort is needed as the grace of God destroys avidyā and allows liberation.

Lastly, Baladeva wrote a commentary on the Brahma-Sūtra based mainly on the doctrines of Madhva and Caitanya. His philosophy is called Acintya Bhedābheda, Unthinkable Dualistic Non-Dualism.

While stating that the difference between saguṇa Brahman and individual souls is real, Baladeva does not make the difference absolute,

---

[28] C. Sharma, p. 379.

as does Madhva, for the effect cannot be absolutely different from the cause.[29] Souls emanate from Brahman like the rays of the sun and are real. The concept of unthinkability reconciles the contradictions that seem to exist in the nature of Brahman.

The soul is eternal, but not, however, an independent agent, as is saguṇa Brahman. In liberation, the soul has union with God and even takes on some divine attributes, but is always different from God and under God's control.

An intense spiritual love of God (bhakti) is the only means of liberation. The enjoyment of this blissful love of God, usually represented as Kṛṣṇa, is based on intuitive, right knowledge of the self, the world, and God.

The four translations of the Brahma-Sūtra with the commentaries of Śaṅkara, Rāmānuja, and Madhva, form the basis for exploration of the concept of spiritual freedom in this paper.

II. Related Literature

We are fortunate to have available a number of reference works relating to the Brahma-Sūtra and to the concept of spiritual freedom. First to be considered are translations of the Upaniṣads, upon which the sūtras are based. Radhakrishnan's The Principal

---

[29] S. Radhakrishnan, p. 101.

Upaniṣads contains eighteen out of one hundred and eight Upaniṣads. He gives the Sanskṛt verse, translation and explanatory material. For comparative purposes, Swami Prabhavananda and Frederick Manchester have a summary of some of the major Upaniṣads. Sri Aurobindo and Rammurti S. Mishra offer detailed translations and interpretations of the Kena and Īśa Upaniṣads.

Also available in small paperback volumes are the Upaniṣad Series published by Sri Ramakrishna Math in Madras. This series is valuable as a word by word translation is given as well as an over-all English rendering of each passage.

A collection of Vedic hymns is offered by Arthur A. Macdonell. Of special interest is Sri Aurobindo's On the Veda. Half of the book is devoted to the hymns; the other half gives a detailed analysis of the "Secret of the Veda," the symbolic and psychological significance behind the Vedas. His analysis is like the discovery of a lost treasure:

> But far more interesting to me was the discovery of a considerable body of profound psychological thought and experience lying neglected in these ancient hymns. And the importance of this element increased in my eyes when I found, first, that the mantras of the Veda illuminated with a clear and exact light psychological experiences of my own for which I had found no sufficient explanation either in European psychology or in the teachings of Yoga or of Vedanta, so far as I was acquainted with them, and secondly, that they shed light on obscure passages and ideas of the Upaniṣads to which, previously, I could attach no exact meaning and gave at the same time a new sense to much in the Puranas. [30]

Readings in a number of Indian classics are given by S.

---

[30] S. Aurobindo, On the Veda (Pondicherry: Sri Aurobindo Ashram, 1964), p. 41.

Radhakrishnan and Charles A. Moore in A Sourcebook in Indian Philosophy. Samples range from the Bhagavad-Gītā, the Mahābhārata, to Cārvāka and Buddhism, to Saṁkhya, Yoga, and Vedānta.

Comprehensive texts giving overviews of Indian thought include: Chandradhar Sharma's A Critical Survey of Indian Philosophy; S. Chatterjee and D. Datta's An Introduction to Indian Philosophy; and P. T. Raju's Idealistic Thought of India. For aid in defining Sanskṛt terms there is Monier-Williams' A Sanskrit-English Dictionary, and J. M. Tyberg's The Language of the Gods. For a description of modern yoga there is Haridas Chaudhuri's Integral Yoga.

A number of articles in magazines and journals refer to the Brahma-Sūtra and spiritual freedom. Some of the authors are Sushil Maitra, Nagaraja Rao, and Haridas Chaudhuri.

Recently, a number of monks from āśrams in India representing advaita vedānta have published translations of early texts. Not only do the treatises offer helpful information about spiritual freedom, but their introductions are often good sources for background material. Examples are: Swami Nityaswarupananda's Aṣṭāvakra Saṁhitā; Swami Madhavananda's Vivekachūḍāmaṇi of Shri Śhaṅkarāchārya; and Swami Nikhilananda's Ātmabodha of Śri Śankarācārya.

A comparison of some of the ideas found in the Brahma-Sūtra to those of Rammurti S. Mishra, a modern scholar, is the focus of one chapter. For this purpose Mishra's two major texts, Textbook of

Yoga Psychology and Fundamentals of Yoga, will be used.

Finally, several modern holy men of India, not previously mentioned, have publications which relate to the topic of liberation. While in the tradition of the Upaniṣads and Brahma-Sūtra, they offer new interpretations and fresh insights. Some of them are: Teachings of Sri Ramakrishna, Swami Vivekananda's Rāja-Yoga, Swami Ramdas' God Experience, The Teachings of Ramana Maharishi, Swami Muktananda's Guru, and Teachings of Sri Satya Sai Baba.

CHAPTER III

MEANING OF SPIRITUAL FREEDOM AS FOUND IN THE BRAHMA-SŪTRA

I. Content of the Brahma-Sūtra

In order to put the description of spiritual freedom in the perspective of Bādarāyaṇa's basic assumptions and beliefs, the contents of the Brahma-Sūtra will be summarized. Particular emphasis is placed on Chapter I, as here the philosophical foundations are presented. An overview in outline form is also given.

The first sūtra, Chapter One, Part One, reads: "Now, therefore, the desire to know Brahman or ultimate reality." According to the commentaries of Śaṅkara as well as others, the "now, therefore," refers to the idea that one desiring to know the absolute Brahman must be morally pure and have his life in order.[1] Further, the results obtained by works and sacrifices are temporary, while the result of knowledge of ultimate reality is eternal. Therefore, the

---

[1] S. Radhakrishnan, The Brahma Sūtra: The Philosophy of Spiritual Life (London: George Allen & Unwin Ltd., 1960), p. 234.

study of Brahman is of great importance and helps one to realize liberation.[2]

While the first sūtra refers to Brahman in the absolute sense,[3] the second discusses Brahman as Īśvara, the creator: "Ultimate reality is that from which proceeds the origin (subsistence and destruction) of the universe." Various interpretations are given by the commentators. For instance, according to Śaṅkara, the universe proceeds from God who is inclusive of both the absolute (nirguṇa) and creative (saguṇa) aspects. Rāmānuja, on the other hand, emphasizes the creative aspect and makes it the highest reality.

The next sūtra states that Brahman is the source of the Vedas. While the mystical experience is not irrational, nevertheless we cannot reach God through logic and inference alone. The scriptures point to the experiences and intuitions of enlightened men and thus show the way to knowledge of Brahman. These men had realized Brahman; therefore Brahman is the source of their message.

The fourth sūtra indicates that Brahman is the main purport of all Vedāntic scriptures. Some of the passages seem to be contradictory, but these differences can be reconciled. Brahman as the

---

[2]Swami Vireswarananda, trans., Brahma-Sutras, by Bādarāyaṇa (Calcutta: Advaita Ashrama, 1970), p. 22.

[3]S. Radhakrishnan, p. 240.

infinite, as creator, as individual soul, is the main subject of all the texts.

These first four sūtras are considered to be the essence of the teaching of the Brahma-Sūtra.

The next section, consisting of sūtras 5-11, refutes the Sāṅkhya arguments that pradhāna or prakṛti is first cause of the universe. Swami Vireswarananda summarizes the Sāṅkhya position:

> The Vedānta texts about creation do not refer to Brahman but to the unintelligent Pradhāna made up of the three gunas . . . Pradhāna has Sattva for one of its components, of which, according to Smriti (Gita 14. 17), knowledge is an attribute. Therefore the Pradhāna can figuratively be said to be omniscient, because of its capacity for all knowledge. To Brahman, on the other hand, which is isolated and pure intelligence itself, you cannot ascribe all-knowingness or partial-knowledge. Moreover, as the Pradhāna has three components, it seems reasonable that it alone is capable of undergoing modifications, like clay, into various objects of name and form, and not Brahman, which is uncompounded, homogeneous, and unchangeable.[4]

The Chāndogya Upaniṣad is particularly referred to in the sūtras to refute these arguments. The first cause is said to have willed or thought the universe into existence and pradhāna cannot do this.[5] Also, it is impossible for an intelligent soul to merge with insentient pradhāna. The "Thou art that" of the sixth chapter of the Chāndogya

---

[4]S. Vireswarananda, p. 32.

[5]Chāndogya Upaniṣad, VI. 2. 2-3.

Upaniṣad and "When a man is said to be asleep, he is united with the Sat, my child--he merges with his own self,"[6] indicates there is an intelligent cause with which the soul realizes its unity. And then, sūtra 11 states that all-knowing Brahman alone is the first cause of this world because "it is known directly from the Vedas."

For the rest of Chapter One, Part One of the Brahma-Sūtra, the discussion relates to God with qualities (saguṇa Brahman) as indicating and as leading the aspirant to God without qualities (nirguṇa Brahman). Although Brahman is one, it can be meditated on and known with, as well as without, qualities. For instance, sūtra 12 states the "blissful one (ānandamaya) is Brahman." Several verses in the Upaniṣads support this conclusion: "He attains the Self full of Bliss"[7] and in "Knowledge, Bliss, Brahman," the word bliss is used for Brahman itself.[8] Other sūtras discuss Upaniṣadic terms as space, prāṇa, light, and life, and conclude that they, too, refer to Brahman.

Up to this point the sūtras discussed terms which definitely relate to Brahman. In the second and third parts of Chapter I, ideas mentioned in the Upaniṣads with no clear reference to Brahman are shown also to be speaking of God. Since God is the cause of all,

---

[6]Chāndogya Upaniṣad, VI. 8. 1.

[7]Taittirīya Upaniṣad, II. 8.

[8]Bṛhad-āraṇyaka Upaniṣad, III. 9. 28.7.

the sūtras infer, he possesses within him all the effects. For instance, in the Chāndogya Upaniṣad the supreme is measured by a span,[9] which appears to be a limitation. The sūtras explain this by saying that while the supreme transcends all limitations, he manifests himself in limited forms. Further elucidation of such passages are given, showing Brahman to be the topic throughout the Upaniṣads.

In the final part of Chapter I, the Sāṅkhya point that prakṛti is first cause of the universe is refuted in great detail.

Thus we see how Bādarāyaṇa established the basis on which the Vedāntic system of thought builds. We can know of Brahman by way of scriptures written by enlightened men; the scriptures have Brahman as their topic; Brahman is the first cause of the universe; and all Sāṇkhya objections are refuted. Next, in Chapter II, proof is further shown that these conclusions are in harmony with sages and texts esteemed through the ages.

One question raised in Chapter II concerns cause and effect, good and evil. Why would the supreme, who is omniscient and omnipotent, create sorrow, cruelty, and negative qualities? In II. 1. 14 the <u>Brahma-Sūtra</u> responds that the world is non-different from the

---

[9] Chāndogya Upaniṣad, V. 18.1.

cause, Brahman. The world cannot exist apart from Brahman. On this subject, Śaṅkara points out that the difference between the world and Brahman, between cause and effect as well as polarities of good and evil, exists only as long as we are not aware of true knowledge. Only our limited perspective, through avidyā, makes polarities as good and evil appear valid.

Śaṅkara does not insist on absolute oneness of the world with Brahman, but does deny that there is any difference. A tree, for instance, is considered in itself, one; yet it has many branches. Unity and multiplicity are both true. In the same way, Brahman has many powers and expresses diversity, yet is one.[10]

The major point of Chapter II is that Brahman created all manifestations. Intelligence, however, is non-produced as it is the nature of Brahman. Also, the soul is uncreated as it is eternal and not divided from Brahman.[11] It only seems different due to limiting adjuncts.

Spiritual practice, states of mind (waking, dreaming, deep sleep), and the soul's travels at physical death are among the topics covered in Chapter III. At physical death, the sūtras state that the soul takes subtle material elements for seeds of a new body. This

---

[10]S. Radhakrishnan, p. 347.

[11]Brahma-Sūtra, II. 3. 17-18.

residual substance determines the nature of a new birth when the soul is ready for another embodiment.[12] Immaculate conception can take place if there is very good karma.[13] Souls can connect with plants, but real re-birth is always in human form.[14]

Chapter III also points out that rituals and practices described in various places in the Upaniṣads, but which have similar purposes, are actually the same and can be combined. This helps the student to reach the essence of the ritual, its symbolic meaning and purpose, without undergoing unnecessary repetition.

In Chapter III, what happens at physical death to the unrealized soul is described. Now, in Chapter IV, details of what happens to a knower of saguṇa Brahman and nirguṇa Brahman are presented. Also, descriptions of meditational techniques to attain liberation are offered.

Much of the last two chapters of the Brahma-Sūtra consider the nature of spiritual freedom, how it is realized, and what happens to the enlightened soul. We now turn to this analysis in more detail.

---

[12] Ibid., III. 1.1-11.

[13] Ibid., III. 1.19.

[14] Ibid., III. 1. 24-27.

FIGURE 1

OUTLINE OF CONTENT OF BRAHMA-SŪTRA

Chapter I — Samanvaya (reconciliation through proper interpretation)		Chapter II — Avirodha (Non-Contradiction)	
Section 1:	Pre-requisite to study of Brahman; Brahman established by means of Vedas and scriptures; all scriptures, despite seeming discrepancies, refer to Brahman; sāṅkhya idea of prakṛti (nature) as creator refuted; scriptural terms (as bliss, prāṇa) refer to Brahman.	Section 1:	All arguments against Brahman as being first cause are refuted. God is ground of unity and multiplicity. Creation proceeds from nature of supreme without any reference to purpose; Līlā (joy overflowing into existence) motivation.
Section 2:	More passages, especially with no clear mention of the characteristics of Brahman, are shown to refer to Brahman.	Section 2:	Inconsistency of non-Vedāntic schools shown. Brahman, himself unmoved, can cause movement in the universe — as an immobile magnet can move an object.
Section 3:	More on various terms in Upaniṣads referring to Brahman.	Section 3:	Harmonizes contradictions in scriptures to uphold doctrine that Brahman is first cause of the universe. Considers whether manifestations are co-eternal with Brahman or issue from it. All manifestations issue from Brahman. Soul and intelligence, however, are not produced; they are eternal and non-divided—may appear different due to limiting adjuncts.
Section 4:	Sāṇkhya objections dealt with.	Section 4:	All senses, organs created by Brahman for enjoyment of the soul.

	Chapter III — Sādhanā (Spiritual Practice)		Chapter IV — Phala (Fruit of Knowledge)
Section 1:	The soul's travels in other planes and at death; residual karma is held in subtle elements for rebirth. Purpose of descriptions is to achieve detachment from world by showing its limitations.	Section 1:	Means to knowledge, cont'd. By destruction of actions which do not yet yield results, a knower of Brahman attains Jīvanmukti; and on exhaustion of prārabdha works, he attains Videhamukti at death and becomes one with Brahman.
Section 2:	Dream state is described. Are dreams caused by individual soul or supreme soul? Śaṅkara says individual soul with limiting adjuncts creates dreams, therefore dreams unreal. Individual soul rests in heart with Brahman during deep, dreamless sleep. Identity of Jīva and Brahman established.	Section 2:	Path of Gods which the knower of Saguṇa Brahman travels is described. Mergence of speech, etc., in mind; mind in prāṇa; prāṇa in fire; fire in highest deity. Final dissolution doesn't take place till knowledge of Nirguṇa Brahman.
Section 3:	Spiritual practices which are described as slightly different in the Upaniṣads are actually one and the same. Those which have different subject matter are separate, although there are similarities. Importance of meditation. Fruit of spiritual practices are the same.	Section 3:	Path itself described. Only worshippers of saguṇa Brahman who don't use symbol of saguṇa Brahman get to Brahmaloka. Knowers of saguṇa Brahman stay in Brahmaloka till its dissolution. Release here is by gradual steps.
Section 4:	Works don't cause knowledge but have a place as means to knowledge of Brahman, as horse used to draw cart but not plough. Indirect. Liberation can't be delayed after knowledge.	Section 4:	Knowers of nirguṇa Brahman: released soul does not acquire new characteristics but manifests its true nature. No need for path or steps or going anywhere. As knower of saguṇa Brahman, there is ability to animate several bodies at the same time; also, has all powers except that of creation; those who go to Brahmaloka do not return to mortal plane unless for some high purpose.

II. Description of Spiritual Freedom in the Brahma-Sūtra

Great care was taken in Chapters I and II of the Brahma-Sūtra to point out the Brahman is the first cause of the universe and all the topics in the Upaniṣads basically refer to Brahman.

Chapter III. 2. 11-30 considers the nature of Brahman, whether God is different or non-different from its manifestations. Unfortunately the sūtras can be interpreted two ways and the commentators have simply been able to choose between them. By selecting III. 2. 25 ("as in the case of light etc. there is no difference between Brahman and its manifestation in activity . . ."), Śaṅkara states there is non-difference between Brahman and Jīva. If the difference were real, Śaṅkara feels that no liberation would be possible. Swami Vireswarananda describes Śaṅkara's view of this sūtra:

> Even as between the sun and its reflection in water etc. there is in reality no difference, the image being unreal, so also the one Brahman manifests as many in the limiting adjuncts of activity like meditation etc. Through ignorance the meditating self thinks it is different from Brahman; but in reality it is identical with Brahman. That it is so is known from repeated instruction of the Sruti in texts like, "That thou art," "I am Brahman," which deny difference.[15]

On the other hand, by selecting III. 2. 27 ("On account of both--i.e. difference and non-difference--being taught, the relation of Jīva and

---

[15] S. Vireswarananda, p. 306.

Brahman is like that between a serpent and its coils"), Rāmānuja claims that God and his creations are like the snake and its coils, both different and non-different from each other.

Liberation for Śaṅkara, then, would mean total non-difference with God whereas for Rāmānuja there would be some difference.

The reason both views can be supported and the Brahma-Sūtra's claim to consistency maintained, lies in the question of whether the individual sūtras represent Bādarāyaṇa's view or the prima facie view. As will be recalled, each topic in the Brahma-Sūtra has within it five factors: subject matter, doubt or uncertainty, statement of objection, established conclusion, and transition to the next topic. So for Śaṅkara, III. 2. 27 is the statement of the objection (prima facie) and for Rāmānuja it is the established conclusion.

Actually, the sūtras' description of liberation itself can be shown to encompass both views. A distinction is made between knowledge of saguṇa Brahman and of nirguṇa Brahman. Sūtras III. 3. 29-31 state that after physical death the knower of manifested Brahman goes along the "path of the Gods" while the knower of unmanifested Brahman does not. It is not necessary for a knower of nirguṇa Brahman to go anywhere but simply realize his non-difference with the absolute. Not much can be said about this state as words themselves presuppose duality. In IV. 4. 1, however, the totally released soul is said to manifest its own nature; nothing new is acquired. The Chāndogya Upaniṣad is referred to: "Now this serene and happy being, after rising from this body, and having attained the highest light, reaches his own true form . . . That is Brahman."[16] The characteristics of a knower of nirguṇa Brahman can be stated as pure intelligence and, from our relative standpoint, qualities as omniscience and omnipotence and freedom from sin and desire.[17]

More is described about the knower of saguṇa Brahman. This type of soul is released by gradual steps. When physical death occurs, the functions of the organs (as speech, hearing, etc.) merge in the mind; the mind merges into prāṇa or life force; prāṇa merges into fire; and fire into the highest deity. (This last mergence into highest deity is not total until knowledge of nirguṇa Brahman is attained.)[18] The soul of the knower of saguṇa Brahman is said to pass through the heart and depart the body from the skull,[19] while the unrealized soul leaves the body in other ways.

The liberated soul then travels to the sun along its rays, encountering various deities as fire, air, wind, Indra, Prajāpati, and finally arrives at Brahmaloka, the place of the Gods.[20] The

---

[16]Chāndogya Upaniṣad, VIII. 3. 4.

[17]Brahma-Sūtra, IV. 4. 5-7. [18]Ibid., IV. 2. 1-6.

[19]Ibid., IV. 2. 17-19 [20]Ibid., IV. 3. 1-6.

highest Brahman is attained only after the passing away of Brahmaloka.[21] Only those who worship Brahman without a symbol can obtain Brahmaloka.[22]

One way of interpreting this symbolic path of the Gods is to say that the released soul travels by way of his enlightened consciousness (the sun's rays) to aspects of divine consciousness to, finally, the place of the Gods.

Some of the characteristics of the knower of saguṇa Brahman include the ability to fulfill the soul's desires by will alone, to choose whether to be embodied or not, and to animate several bodies at once.[23] In fact, the sūtras state the released soul has all powers of God, except that of creation, preservation, and destruction of the world.[24]

However, if oneness with nirguṇa Brahman is attained, there can be no limitations.[25] As Radhakrishnan puts it:

> The Supreme Lord abides in two forms, the transcendental and the empirical. He who worships the Lord in his empirical aspect does not attain his transcendental form. Since the worshipper is able to comprehend him only partially, he attains only limited powers and not unlimited powers like the Lord himself.[26]

---

[21] Ibid., IV. 3. 10.

[22] Ibid., IV. 3. 15-16.

[23] Ibid., IV. 4. 8-16.

[24] Ibid., IV. 4. 17.

[25] Ibid., IV. 4. 19

[26] S. Radhakrishnan, p. 561.

Thus we see how Śaṅkara's conception of the non-difference of Jīva and Brahman is substantiated by the Brahma-Sūtra's description of nirguṇa Brahman; and Rāmānuja's stance of difference and non-difference is supported by the description of the manifested Brahman. Rāmānuja claims that we can never totally realize nirguṇa Brahman; and from the relative standpoint one can imagine Śaṅkara agreeing.

However Śaṅkara and Rāmānuja start from the same texts and assumptions, they come to different conclusions:

> Rāmānuja concentrates his attention on the relation of the world to God, and argues that God is indeed real and independent; but the souls of the world are real also, though their reality is utterly dependent on that of God . . . He insists on the continued individual existence of the released souls . . . matter and souls have existence only as the body of Brahman, i.e. they can exist and be what they are simply because Brahman is their soul and controlling power . . So Rāmānuja's theory is an advaita or non-dualism, though with a qualification (viśeṣa), viz. that it admits plurality, since the supreme spirit subsists in a plurality of forms as soul and matter.[27]

Rāmānuja's stance emphasizes devotion to God as the path to liberation and Śaṅkara's followers often emphasized knowledge and right understanding. Both these viewpoints are found in the Brahma-Sūtra.

To form a more complete picture of the various ways the concept of spiritual freedom in the Brahma-Sūtra has been interpreted,

---

[27]S. Radhakrishnan, Indian Philosophy, II (New York: The Macmillan Company, 1962), p. 660.

Madhva, as a representative of the dualistic viewpoint, should be mentioned. Madhva matintains there is total difference between God and his creation. He quotes IV. 4. 17 ("The released soul has all lordly powers, except creation . . .") as showing there will always be separation between Jīva and Brahman. In fact, for Madhva there are five basic distinctions. These exist between God and the individual soul, God and matter, soul and matter, one soul and another, and finally, between one point of matter and another.[28]

Liberation, for Madhva, can only mean being close to God. He describes four kinds of liberation: entrance of freed souls into the body of God; residence in heaven with continual sight of God; residence near God; and attendants to God.[29]

Regardless of which definition of spiritual freedom one feels to be closest to the intent of the Brahma-Sūtra, two other questions arise: when does enlightenment occur, and what methods are recommended for its attainment?

Very clearly the sūtras state that right knowledge of Brahman results immediately in liberation.[30] The soul needs a body to undergo the disciplines which it takes to attain knowledge.[31] Right knowledge

---

[28] S. Radhakrishnan, Indian Philosophy, p. 738.

[29] S. Radhakrishnan, Brahma-Sūtra, p. 65.

[30] Brahma-Sutra, I. 1. 1.; III. 4. 1.; III. 3. 28.

[31] Ibid., III. 3. 28.

can occur in this life. However, if there are results of some previous actions (karma) which are currently reaching maturity, right knowledge will arise in the next life.[32] When, finally, all works which had begun to bear fruit are exhausted, knowledge is attained and the soul realizes its oneness with Brahman.[33]

Good works, rituals, and spiritual practices do not cause right knowledge, but they do purify the mind to make its reception possible.[34] In sūtra III. 4. 26. the example of a horse is given. The horse does not till the field, but pulls the plough. In the same way, works cause knowledge only indirectly.

The sūtras recommend meditation of Brahman to obtain release. In III. 3., various meditations are prescribed. Since it is difficult for the ordinary man to meditate on the absolute, symbols of Brahman such as prāṇa, ākāśa, and the mind are suggested as objects to meditate on. Different methods mentioned in the Vedas, but having basically the same subject, are combined into a single meditation.

Meditations which are practices for knowledge of Brahman all have the same result. But the individual should select one form of meditation and continue with it until the fruit of the meditation is realized. Change from one form of meditation to another distracts

---

[32] Ibid., III. 4. 51.

[33] Ibid., IV. 1. 19.

[34] Ibid., III. 4. 1.

the mind.[35] The sūtras encourage the use of Aum.[36]

Meditation on the self as Brahman should be repeated until right knowledge is attained. When symbols are used, the caution is given not to identify with the symbols. For instance, if the mind as Brahman is used, the meditator should not identify with the mind. Also, the mind should be meditated on as Brahman, not Brahman as the mind. The suggestion here is to look on all symbols as manifestations of the supreme, not the other way around. The attempt is to reach first cause. Continue to meditate until physical death, the sūtras advise, as whatever is believed and understood, that will be attained.[37] We make our own reality up to the level of our understanding; we become what we meditate on.

III. Reference to Spiritual Freedom in the Īśa and Kena Upaniṣads

The Brahma-Sūtra bases its aphorisms on all the Upaniṣads. It is well, then, to consider briefly at least two of the major texts to see if they are in harmony with the concept of spiritual freedom in the Brahma-Sūtra. The Īśa and Kena Upaniṣads were chosen for this purpose.

---

35 Ibid., 3.59. 36 Ibid., 4.22. 37 Ibid., 1.1-12.

As with all the major Upaniṣads, the Īśa and Kena have as their main concern the movement from ignorance and suffering to knowledge and bliss.[38]

The Īśa Upaniṣad teaches the essential unity of pure consciousness with the manifested universe. Man, as a knower of saguṇa Brahman, can be aware that all is God and yet can concurrently be an active, non-attached participant in the world. The first verse sets this theme: "(Know that) all this, whatever moves in this moving world, is enveloped by God. Therefore find your enjoyment in renunciation; do not covet what belongs to others."[39] Thus whatever we come in contact with, as motion and immutability, God and nature, enjoyment and suffering, all are one in Brahman. We are asked to become non-attached to egoistic desires, to see all as belonging to God. Gandhi comments on this verse:

> Since God pervades everything, nothing belongs to you, not even your own body. God is the undisputed, unchallengable Master of everything you possess. If it is universal brotherhood--not only brotherhood of all human beings, but of all living things--I find it in this _mantra_ . . . Since he pervades every fiber of my being and of all of

---

[38]Sri Aurobindo, _Kena Upaniṣad_ (Pondicherry: Sri Aurobindo Ashrama, 1970), p. 15.

[39]S. Radhakrishnan, _The Principal Upaniṣads_, (London: George Allen & Unwin Ltd., 1955), p. 567.

> you, I derive from it the doctrine of equality of all creatures on earth . . .[40]

The second mantra in the Īśa Upaniṣad continues the idea of selfless service. In fact, only with such an attitude does liberation become a possibility:

> Always performing unselfish services in this world, one should wish to live for a hundred years. If you live in this way, O man, and practice meditation and without any ulterior motive serve all beings, you will perceive the Supreme, and your own karmas will not bind you. There is no other way than this by which you will experience the Supreme and by which your karmas will not adhere to you.[41]

This total dropping of the egotistic standpoint is obviously a difficult task for man, necessitating a change of feeling, thinking, and total life orientation. Man should live in the world and serve, but without attachments to results.

It is not good to neglect spiritual studies for the world, nor to neglect the world for spirituality. Each is a part of the other and cannot be separated. Supreme consciousness is essentially one, but has two aspects: unity and multiplicity. Verse 9 elaborates on this:

> Into blinding darkness enter those who are absorbed in the analysis of . . . the relative universe alone. But those who delight in spiritual practice alone . . . enter into a still greater darkness, as it were.[42]

---

[40] Ibid., p. 568.

[41] Rammurti S. Mishra, Īśa Upaniṣad (Dayton, Ohio: Yoga Society, 1962), p. 8.

[42] Ibid., p. 24.

Perhaps the most definitive statement on the non-duality of man and Brahman is found in Verse 16:

> O Pūṣan, the sole seer, O Controller, O Sun, offspring of Prajā-pati, spread forth your rays and gather up your radient light that I may behold you of lovliest form. Whosoever is that person (yonder) that also am I.[43]

Both a prayer and a statement, the verse affirms that the entire universe is the manifestation of the Supreme. As Mishra states:

> This Mantra declares eternal unity and identity of the "I" Principle behind the individual as well as the universal existence. The manifestations of the individual as well as the universal existence apparently divide and multiply the soul into infinite numbers of selves while in Reality the Supreme Self, the I AM remains One-without-a-second.[44]

To the ancient sages, Sūrya, the sun, represents divine consciousness and Agni, fire, is divine will.[45] In the last verse of the Īśa Upanisad, Agni is called upon to guide us to spiritual prosperity. Here the reference is to the path of the Gods[46] described in the Brahma-Sūtra. The symbolism of these passages, then, implies that surrender to divine will can lead us to knowledge of Brahman and enlightenment.

---

[43]S. Radhakrishnan, The Principal Upaniṣads, p. 577.

[44]R. S. Mishra, p. 41.

[45]Sri Aurobindo, Isha Upanishad (Pondicherry: Sri Aurobindo Ashram, 1973), pp. 66-67.

[46]R. S. Mishra, p. 45.

The Īśa Upaniṣad concerns itself with the relationship between Brahman and the whole world of manifestation while the Kena Upaniṣad particularly discusses the relation of mind to Brahman consciousness. The first two chapters of the Kena deal with the supreme as nirguṇa Brahman, and the last two with Īśvara or saguṇa Brahman.

Describing the supreme, states the Kena Upaniṣad, is beset with difficulties: "There sight travels not, nor speech, nor the mind. We know It not nor can distinguish how one should teach It . . ."[47] and "I think not that I know It well, and yet I know that It is not unknown to me."[48] Although Brahman is the essence of our being, we cannot know it objectively. True knowledge is not found in the mind, senses, speech, or their objects, but in the supreme which forms these instruments and is independent of them. We are told to study and meditate on the essence behind all these manifestations:

> That which is not thought by mindstuff but that by which, they say, mindstuff is thought--that alone know as Brahman, not this that people worship here.[49]

In the third and fourth chapters, various gods representing man's material, vital, and mental functions are shown to be dependent

---

[47] Kena Upaniṣad, I. 3.

[48] Ibid., II. 2.

[49] Ibid., I. 6.

on Brahman. Of themselves, they have no power. If a man experiences victory over evil tendencies within himself, he cannot be proud or feel as though he deserves the credit. The victory is due to God alone.

> This is the truth of Brahman in relation to nature: whether in the flash of the lightning, or in the wink of eyes, the power that is shown is the power of Brahman. This is the truth of Brahman in relation to man: in the motions of the mind, the power that is shown is the power of Brahman.[50]

The last verse of the Kena Upaniṣad indicates that one who truly understands this teaching will shake off all sins and become established in the highest reality. Again we are told to meditate on Brahman alone.

Kena means "by whom." This upaniṣad asks the basic question: Who causes our mind, energy, and senses to act? The answer is Brahman. The purpose of the upaniṣad is to show the unity of individual consciousness with supreme consciousness.

The idea of spiritual freedom found in the Brahma-Sūtra can be seen to be in harmony with these two upaniṣads. The non-duality of Brahman and manifestation is established.[51] True knowledge

---

[50]Swami Prabhavananda and Frederick Manchester, The Upanishads (New York: The New American Library, 1948), pp. 32-3.

[51]Brahma-Sūtra, II. 1. 14; III. 2. 25; Īśa, 16; Kena, I. 5.

allows the soul to realize liberation.[52] Selfless service helps to purify the mind and indirectly causes right knowledge.[53] The path of the Gods is indicated in the Īśa Upanisad and described in detail in the Brahma-Sūtra. Meditation on the highest Brahman is recommended to realize knowledge and liberation.

The purpose of the upaniṣads and the Brahma-Sūtra is identical: to know God, to realize the unity of the Supreme and its individual expression and to thus attain spiritual freedom.

---

[52] Brahma-Sūtra, III. 4. 52.; Īśa, 11; Kena, IV. 9.

[53] Brahma-Sūtra III. 4. 26.; Īśa, 2; Kena, IV. 8.

CHAPTER IV

THE CONCEPT OF SPIRITUAL FREEDOM IN THE BRAHMA-SŪTRA RELATED TO A CONTEMPORARY SCHOLAR

In the west today there are many philosophers who attempt to bring man closer to self-realization and liberation. Examples, both psychologically and theologically oriented, are almost overwhelming in their numbers: Krishnamurti, Roberto Assagioli, and Teilhard de Chardin are but a few. As Jacob Needleman states in The New Religions:

> The number of Americans engaged in some sort of spiritual discipline is impressive enough. When we add to that number those who now seek to guide their lives simply by the ideas associated by these traditions, we cannot avoid the picture of a "spiritual explosion."[1]

To choose one out of the many who have contributed to this subject is a somewhat arbitrary decision. Dr. Rammurti S. Mishra was chosen as in addition to his knowledge of Indian philosophy, he has a background in modern medical science. Born in India and raised in a Brahmin family, he studied Sanskṛt and became a priest in

---

[1]Jacob Needleman, The New Religions (New York: Doubleday and Company, 1970), p. 194.

Advaita Vedānta. Also a medical doctor and psychiatrist, he practiced in India, England, Canada, and the United States, and thus expresses a synthesis of Vedic tradition and twentieth-century psychiatry.

In addition to this synthesis, Mishra also represents a blending of Vedānta and Sāṅkhya philosophies. As a priest in Advaita Vedānta, he has studied the ideas of Śaṅkara, who founded the Advaita Vedānta mutts or monasteries in the ninth century. He has also studied with teachers of the Sāṅkhya philosophy and his Textbook of Yoga Psychology is based on Patañjali's Yoga Sūtras and Sāṅkhya. It will be of value to see how Mishra distinguishes and blends these two philosophies and then to compare his ideas to the Brahma-Sūtra.

Four branches of Sāṅkhya are described by Mishra: 1) Kapila's Sāṅkhya, based on the Vedas and Upaniṣads, allows saguṇa Brahman in relativity and nirguṇa Brahman or monism beyond relativity, exactly as Vedānta; 2) Theistic Sāṅkhya, found in the Mahābhārata, Gītā, Purāṇas, emphasizes the relative differences between puruṣa (eternal, conscious, supreme self) and prakṛti (eternal, unconscious cause of the world of relativity, supreme nature); 3) the Sāṅkhya system in the Buddhist period was atheistic, and based on logical deduction; 4) Theistic Sāṅkhya was again emphasized in the 16th century.[2]

---

[2] Rammurti S. Mishra, The Textbook of Yoga Psychology (New York: The Julian Press, Inc., 1971), pp. 4-5.

Theistic Sāṅkhya is discussed in Textbook of Yoga Psychology. Two fundamental realities are postulated: puruṣa and prakṛti. Puruṣa is subject, conscious witness; prakṛti is object, unconscious cause of the world. Throughout theistic Sāṅkhya, these two elements are treated as eternally separate and as having totally different functions.

While following the Sāṅkhya system, Mishra additionally points out the ultimate interdependence of puruṣa and prakṛti. Prakṛti is the energy behind puruṣa;[3] puruṣa is the light of consciousness which illuminates prakṛti.[4]

> Likewise, if Purusa and prakriti are parallel, ultimate realities, then we must investigate a third force of which these are two aspects. Without some intimate relationship, these two cannot stand together. How can Conscious Purusa and unconscious prakriti be united? . . . Really speaking, post-Buddhistic, dualistic Samkhya summarized wonderfully all the elements of the universe into two fundamental principles of Conscious Energy and unconscious energy, but ultimately failed to bring out their real relationship . . .
>
> Without association with prakriti, Purusa cannot become omnipotent and, without the association with Purusa, prakriti by itself cannot become systematic and intelligent. Hence the meeting point of these two mighty energies is called Brahman. Brahman is simultaneously immanent and transcendent. In short, Purusa and prakriti are two aspects of the One Ultimate Reality, which has neither name nor form and technically is called Brahman.[5]

---

[3]Ibid., p. 107. [4]Ibid., p. 28. [5]Ibid., pp. 57-8.

It will be remembered that in the Brahma-Sūtra much effort was given to denouncing the Sāṅkhya idea that prakṛti, and not Brahman, is creator of the manifested world. While it was undoubtedly important for Bādarāyaṇa to clarify this issue, a synthesis of Vedānta with Sāṅkhya, rather than a polarized rejection, is possible. If puruṣa and prakṛti are two aspects of Brahman, then Brahman can be said ultimately to have been the "causeless cause" of creation.

Other points of difference between Sāṅkhya and Vedānta can be noted. For instance, Sāṅkhya suggests the existence of many selves, rather than one universal self pervading all bodies alike, as Advaita Vedānta states.[6] If everyone had the same self within, Sāṅkhya reasons, then all would have exactly the same life experiences. Madhva, of Dualistic Vedānta, uses much the same reasoning: if all selves were identical, there would be no difference between a liberated soul and an unliberated one.[7]

Mishra suggests the difference may not be as acute as it seems on the surface. Cittam, the individual's perceptual mechanism or mindstuff, continually undergoes modifications and thus makes the self appear to change.[8]

---

[6]S. Chatterjee and D. Datta, An Introduction to Indian Philosophy (Calcutta: University of Calcutta, 1968), p. 266.

[7]S. Radhakrishnan, The Brahma-Sūtra (London: George Allen & Unwin Ltd., 1960), p. 63.

[8]R.S. Mishra, p. 63.

> Individual souls are fundamentally identical in nature with Absolute Purusa and identical among themselves. Differences are due to the physical organization that separates an individual soul from other individual souls and from Absolute Purusa, Brahman. The nature of bodies and mindstuff through which Self is incorporated is responsible for various degrees of limitations. Individuality is due to the individual mechanism of perception, individual mindstuff. When individual mindstuff is analyzed, it is transformed into Cosmic Mindstuff, and Absolute Purusa, free from all accidents of finite life and above time and change, is realized.[9]

Sāṅkhya's dualism and difference from Advaita Vedānta's interpretation of the Brahma-Sūtra has been noted in two ways: the separation of puruṣa and prakṛti, and the postulate of the existence of many selves. Also noted was Mishra's acceptance of dualism as far as it goes, along with his point that ultimate Brahman includes both prakṛti and puruṣa; further, all souls are fundamentally identical with Brahman and with each other. Thus a blend of Vedānta and Sāṅkhya is achieved.

One value of Sāṅkhya is found in its systematic approach to the study of mind and matter in regard to attainment of spiritual freedom. As Mishra states:

> Psychological analysis begins in dualistic experiences and ends in identity and non-dualistic knowledge.[10]

---

[9]Ibid., pp. 345-6. [10]Ibid., p. 59.

The Yoga Sūtras of Patañjali are the practical application of Sāṅkhya theory and are based on principles regarded as psychologically sound today as when they were written centuries ago. Consideration will now be given to some of Mishra's commentaries on these principles to see how they relate to the concept of spiritual freedom in the <u>Brahma-Sūtra.</u>

Mishra states, as did the <u>Brahma-Sūtra,</u> that ignorance is the cause of bondage and knowledge allows liberation. Further, liberation is the individual's realization of non-duality with Brahman:

> <u>Ātman</u> is the reality of individual self. . . It is identical with <u>Purusa</u>, <u>Brahman.</u> It is one eternal, universal Consciousness. It is never in bondage. It is eternally liberated, nityamukta. <u>Ātman</u> is eternally shining with its own light and radiating with its own eternal energy. The feeling of bondage is due to ignorance of its existence, consciousness, and bliss. Due to this ignorance, individual self identifies with the body. . . <u>Avidyā,</u> nescience, ignorance, is the cause of bondage. It is intellectual knowledge infected with the duality of subject and object. <u>Avidyā</u> is removed by intuitive knowledge of <u>vidyā</u>, by which individual self obtains identity of its existence, consciousness, and bliss with Universal Existence, Consciousness, and Bliss of <u>Puruṣa</u>, <u>Brahman.</u> This <u>vidyā</u>, true insight, integral experience, leads to <u>liberation.</u> Ignorance itself is bondage and knowledge itself is liberation.[11]

Bondage and ignorance are due to identification with materiality. It is not so much the material world which causes suffering, but rather the false identification of spirit with matter. Identification with body and senses causes suffering.[12] As a house is for a man,

---

[11] Ibid., p. 373.

[12] Ibid., p. 284.

not a man for a house, so matter is for the self, not self for matter. Yet on the plane of relativity, they are both needed. We should not disregard or negate the material world, we need only learn not to identify with it.[13]

While the Brahma-Sūtra focuses on the philosophical implications of man's relationship to God, Mishra in his textbook emphasizes the process of self-analysis to realize spiritual freedom. Thus detailed description is given of the nature of the mind. To discriminate the self from the not-self, we must have knowledge of how the body and mind work. Cittam, the perceptual mechanism or mindstuff, which we attempt to purify, has three major aspects:

1) manah मनः --instincts (like a government's parliament;)

2) ahaṁkāra अहंकार --self-analytical thought (like the president;)

3) buddhi बुद्धि --conscience, values (like the Supreme Court).[14]

Stemming from manah are the five organs of cognition (hearing, touch, sight, taste, and smell), and the five organs of cognition (hands, feet, speech, excretory, and reproductive).

All manifestation is dependent on the activity of the guṇas and cittam is no exception. Sattva is the predominant guṇa here.

---

[13]Ibid., p. 251. [14]Ibid., p. 107.

Increase of satoguṇa increases knowledge and happiness. But the enlightened state transcends all guṇas and the "flawless flow of consciousness penetrates all subjects and objects of the universe."[15]

When cittam is purified by overcoming barriers and limiting adjuncts, pure consciousness is experienced. The eight steps of Yoga are suggested as means of purification:

1) yama यम --restraints

2) niyama नियम --ethical and moral disciplines

3) āsana आसन --exercises and postures

4) prāṇāyāma प्राणायाम --transformation to cosmic energy

5) pratyāhāra प्रत्याहार --sublimation of psychic energy

6) dhāraṇā धारणा --fixation of mind

7) dhyāna ध्यान --suggestion

8) samādhi समाधि --perception and union with Cosmic Consciousness.[16]

When these last three operate simultaneously, it is called samyama--संयम.[17] With samyama on the aspect of cosmic consciousness, all the senses follow this sustained focus "as an army follows a general," and latent desires disappear.[18]

---

[15]Ibid., pp. 24-5. [16]Ibid., p. 198.

[17]Ibid., p. 226. [18]Ibid., p. 270.

The practice of listening to nādam-- नादम् , the sound current within, is another recommendation for purification of consciousness. It removes mental and physical defects and is said to be "like a hunter which kills animal tendencies of mind."[19] Still another suggestion is to become aware of the "I" in cittam; if one can catch this "I" and remain still with it, the limited "I" of the body, senses, and mind will be annihilated.[20]

Ways to overcome destructive drives are given:

> 1/Defense reaction, by which the mind takes an attitude directly contrary to the impulse and tries to shut it out. 2/Substitution, by which the mind takes up a consciously counter-acting impulse . . .
> 3/Sublimation. The ultimate aim of Yoga is to bring about complete transformation and sublimation of mind-stuff into the light of Purusa, Brahman.[21]

Meditation, use of mantra, devotion, and love are all purifying actions.[22] Also emphasized is the value of understanding all objects, including matter, energy, consciousness, law, and bliss, as the manifestation of the supreme.[23]

The highest goal in life in union with puruṣa, Brahman. One must pass through saguṇa puruṣa, progressing in awareness of existence, knowledge, and bliss, to reach the ultimate nirguṇa puruṣa

---

[19]Ibid., p. 274. [20]Ibid., p. 191.

[21]Ibid., p. 203. [22]Ibid., p. 179. [23]Ibid., p. 323.

or Brahman. "Without Saguna Purusa, Nirguna Purusa cannot be realized directly by human consciousness. Whenever Nirguna Purusa is realized, it is realized by means of the three attributes of Saguna Purusa, Existence, Knowledge, and Reality."[24] Saguṇa Brahman teaches and liberates; in nirguṇa Brahman the individual is identical with the self. Man does not obtain truth, he becomes it.

When this happens, various freedoms are realized. There is freedom from suffering, the pressure of the guṇas is terminated, and the authority of cittam over self is ended.[25] The function of prakṛti is not ended with the enlightenment of an individual, but the play of prakṛti is over for him.[26]

Mishra's concept of spiritual freedom is thus seen to be identical with Śaṅkara's interpretation of the Brahma-Sūtra. Liberation means absolute non-duality with Brahman. This non-duality exists eternally in every soul. Limiting adjuncts only make the individual appear different from Brahman and from other individual souls. Right knowledge and purification remove these barriers.

The Sāṅkhya view of puruṣa and prakṛti has been incorporated by Mishra into the Advaita Vedānta position. Thus much of the Brahma-Sūtra's argument that prakṛti cannot be cause of the world is shown

---

[24]Ibid., p. 372. [25]Ibid., pp. 196-7. [26]Ibid., p. 363.

to be true only if the ultimate unity of puruṣa and prakṛti is not acknowledged.

One of Mishra's major purposes in his commentary on the Yoga Sūtras is to indicate specific psychological methods to remove barriers to liberation. Drawing on his background in psychiatry and medicine, he discusses how the mind functions and gives techniques in self-analysis which can lead to spiritual freedom. While the *Brahma-Sūtra* mentions similar techniques, its emphasis is predominantly philosophical.

CHAPTER V

SUMMARY AND CONCLUSIONS

I. Summary

The basic problem raised at the outset of this paper concerned the implications of spiritual freedom as presented in the *Brahma-Sūtra* and how these ideas apply to us today. The search in our lives for meaning and purpose raises questions about our relationship to God and the world, as well as an understanding of what is meant by the ultimate goal of man's experience--liberation.

The *Brahma-Sūtra* was chosen to study the concept of spiritual freedom as it provides a synthesis and summary of the Upaniṣads and is considered a major treatise by Indian philosophers. Written in the second century A.D. by Bādarāyaṇa, it is composed of 555 aphorisms, many of which are so concise that their meaning is obscured. Further, the division of topics into subject matter, doubts, objections, conclusion, and transition to the next subject has left some confusion as to which sūtra stated the objection and which the conclusion. However Bādarāyaṇa may have been clear about the import of his message, what has reached us today is open to various interpretations.

Before reviewing the major commentators, it is helpful to look at the content of the Brahma-Sūtra. First of all, the Vedas and Upaniṣads are established as valid scriptural authority. The sūtras attempt to show that all scriptures, despite seeming differences, refer to Brahman. Brahman is established as creator of the universe and Sāṅkhya notions of duality are refuted. Every manifestation, including senses and organs, are shown to issue from Brahman. The soul and intelligence, however, are said to be non-produced; they are eternal and indivisible. Līlā motivation, or joy overflowing into existence, is the reason given for creation.

Soul travel after physical death, the transfer of residual karma for rebirth, as well as states of consciousness (waking, dream, dreamless sleep) are covered in the sūtras. Spiritual practices found in the Upaniṣads are consolidated and meditation is stressed.

One of the major points the sūtras make is that right knowledge is necessary to realize liberation. Works by themselves do not bring forth knowledge, but they have an indirect effect by purifying the mind. If a soul has unfinished karma, this must be taken care of before right knowledge occurs.

A detailed description of the path of a knower of saguṇa Brahman (God with qualities) is given: speech and such functions merge into mind, mind into prāṇa, prāṇa into fire, and fire into highest deity. Knowers of saguṇa Brahman stay in Brahmaloka till its dissolution and release is by gradual steps.

According to the sūtras, a knower of saguṇa Brahman can animate several bodies at once and has all powers except that of creation. A knower of nirguṇa Brahman (God without qualities) does not acquire new characteristics nor follow the path to Brahmaloka. Since identity with nirguṇa Brahman implies no manifestation of qualities, the state is indescribable; words and images have no value in the attempt to understand it.

Although the sūtras indicate that the fruit of true knowledge is always liberation, the distinction made between a knower of saguṇa Brahman and of nirguṇa Brahman has contributed to the difference of opinion among commentators. Thus different descriptions of spiritual freedom are given.

Śaṅkara contends that the world is non-dual or identical with Brahman. Liberation is the realization of the identity of the self and Brahman. Nothing new is created but the truth of non-duality is recognized. This total non-duality implies oneness with the absolute, nirguṇa Brahman. Śaṅkara selects sūtra III. 2. 25 ("as in the case of light etc., there is no difference between Brahman and its manifestation in activity . . .") as proving this point.

The world of multiplicity is due to māyā, the creative power of Brahman. When Brahman takes form, its true nature is veiled and we fail to recognize God as existing in all. One who attains spiritual freedom is able to enjoy the play of māyā without being deceived about its true nature.

Śaṅkara recognized the value of relative knowledge and felt that it can lead to absolute knowledge. The way to realize the ultimate is through purification of thought and action, selfless service, and the development of sattvic qualities as harmony, joy, and devotion. Right knowledge is the direct cause of liberation; development of these qualities is the indirect cause of knowledge.

Rāmānuja is another major commentator on the Brahma-Sūtra. He believed, as did Śaṅkara, in the validity of one substance. But unlike Śaṅkara's monism, Rāmāuja felt that this all-inclusive substance exists in two real forms: finite souls and matter. While the soul is eternal, it is not infinite and can never be totally identical with Brahman.

He rejects the idea of one substance which appears as two due to ignorance, as with the advaita vedānta theory of māyā. He also rejects the idea that one substance becomes two in evolution.

Spiritual freedom for Rāmāuja means fellowship with God. Released souls have all the perfections of Brahman except in two points: the soul is atomic in size while spirit is all pervading, and the soul does not have the power of creating, sustaining, and dissolving the world. Individuality is retained with this conceptual framework. Rāmānuja points to sūtra III. 2. 27 ("On account of both--i.e. difference and non-difference--being taught, the relation of Jīva and Brahman is like that between a serpent and its coils") as confirming his theory. Rāmānuja holds that this sūtra is the conclusion of the topic while Śaṅkara feels it is the statement of objection or prima facie view. Thus both conclusions can be supported in the Brahma-Sūtra.

Rāmānuja accepts a theistic view of God with all good qualities or saguṇa Brahman. When all karmas are extinguished by devotion to God, then liberation or closeness to Brahman is attained.

Śaṅkara and Rāmānuja have varying perspectives on man's relationship to God. Although Rāmānuja believes man is the same essence as Brahman, nevertheless there are always some differences. The analogy is given that although a cow is one, it has many parts. In the same way man is a part of God, but never identical with the totality. This difference is not simply due to māyā, but exists eternally. On the other hand, Śaṅkara believed in the non-duality of man and Brahman; the appearance of differences is due to māyā. When true knowledge is realized, man experiences his oneness with the absolute.

These two opinions are actually quite close. Śaṅkara does not deny the validity of God with qualities; in fact he wrote many devotional hymns which could imply a separation between man and Brahman. But ultimately this separation can be transcended, Śaṅkara felt, and nirguṇa Brahman is experienced. Rāmānuja's system emphasizes saguṇa Brahman and claims we can never really experience the absolute. Both viewpoints find support in the Brahma-Sūtra.

Madhva is the third commentator of the Brahma-Sūtra considered and represents a dualistic viewpoint. He believes Brahman to be creator of the universe, yet totally different from creation. In fact, he notes five basic distinctions between God and the individual soul, God and matter, the soul and matter, one soul and another, and between one part of matter and another.

Spiritual freedom can only mean being close to God. The soul is eternal and there are four states of liberation: entrance into God's own body; the soul which is an attendant to God; one which has continual sight of God; and, finally, residence near God. Madhva quotes the Brahma-Sūtra IV. 4. 17 ("The released soul has all lordly powers, except creation . . .") as showing the separation of Brahman and the individual soul.

Śaṅkara, Rāmānuja, and Madhva represent three major interpretations of spiritual freedom in the Brahma-Sūtra. In considering these commentators, the varieties of conclusions possible from this text are shown. However, especially with Śaṅkara and Rāmānuja, some differences seem based on whether the emphasis is given to saguṇa or nirguṇa Brahman.

Bādarāyaṇa based his aphorisms on all the Upaniṣads, which also lend themselves to various interpretations depending on the reader's level of awareness and temperament. It is well to examine two major Upaniṣads to see how their statements on spiritual freedom compare with those found in the Brahma-Sūtra. The Īśa and Kena Upaniṣads were chosen for this purpose.

Both the Īśa and Kena Upaniṣads concern themselves with the removal of ignorance for realization of spiritual freedom. The Īśa discusses the relationship of Brahman and the world of manifestation. Everything is enveloped in God, including polarities as immutability and motion, enjoyment and suffering. We are asked in the first verse to find contentment in renunciation, in the realization that nothing belongs to us personally. All is Brahman. Selfless service in the world is as important as spiritual studies; each is a part of the other and cannot be separated. The point is made that since all is Brahman, the realized soul does not isolate himself from the world but serves without attachment to results or for personal gain.

"Kena" means "by whom" in Sanskṛt. In the Kena Upaniṣad the question is raised: Who causes our mind, energy, and senses to act? Brahman is the answer given; the unity of individual and supreme consciousness is the focal point of this Upaniṣad.

The purpose of these two Upaniṣads and of the Brahma-Sūtra is the same: to know God, to realize the unity of the supreme and manifestation, and to thus attain spiritual freedom. True knowledge allows the experience of liberation; selfless service helps to purify the mind and indirectly causes knowledge. Meditation on the highest Brahman is recommended to realize knowledge and liberation; the path of the Gods is mentioned in the Īśa Upaniṣad and described in the Brahma-Sūtra. The non-duality of Brahman and manifestation is established, thus supporting Śaṅkara's and Rāmānuja's theory of one essence pervading all. As pointed out earlier, Śaṅkara emphasized oneness with nirguṇa Brahman while Rāmānuja suggested a qualified relationship with saguṇa Brahman.

The concept of spiritual freedom in the Brahma-Sūtra has been looked at, as have the commentators and two Upaniṣads. In order to ascertain the relevance of the sūtras to modern thought, consideration was given to Dr. Rammurti S. Mishra. Raised in India, he is a samnyāsin in Advaita Vedānta as well as a medical doctor. His work also represents a synthesis of Sāṅkhya and Vedānta philosophies.

It will be remembered that the Brahma-Sūtra refuted in detail the Sāṅkhya theory that prakṛti created manifestation. In his Textbook of Yoga Psychology based on Patañjali's Yoga sūtras, Mishra points out several interpretations of Sāṅkhya. Among them are Kapila's Sāṅkhya which allows saguṇa Brahman in relativity and nirguṇa Brahman or monism beyond relativity. Also, there is theistic Sāṇkhya which postulates two eternal realities: puruṣa and prakṛti. It is theistic Sāṇkhya which Mishra discusses in his textbook. But Mishra states that puruṣa and prakṛti are ultimately interdependent and that "the meeting point of these two mighty energies is called Brahman. Brahman is simultaneously immanent and transcendent." Thus the duality of Sāṅkhya is overcome if ultimate unity of puruṣa and prakṛti is acknowledged.

Another point of difference between Sāṅkhya and Śaṅkara's interpretation of Vedānta was noted. Sāṅkhya suggests the existence of many selves, rather than one universal self pervading all. If all were identical, Sāṅkhya reasons, every self would have exactly the same experiences.

Mishra attempts a reconciliation of the difference by pointing out that cittam, the perceptual mechanism in man, undergoes modifications and thus makes the self appear to change. Fundamentally, individual souls are identical with the absolute and with each other. Changes exist in relative cittam only. Māyā, the creative power of Brahman, causes form and thus veils Brahman.

Mishra's concept of liberation is seen to be the same as Śaṅkara's interpretation of the Brahma-Sūtra. Spiritual freedom is realization of non-duality with Brahman. This is the soul's eternal, true nature; the limiting adjuncts of cittam only make the self appear to change. Right knowledge removes these barriers.

In relating the Brahma-Sūtra to modern thought, Mishra offers psychological techniques for purification of the mind. For instance, he discusses three ways to overcome destructive drives: defense reactions, substitution, and sublimination. Descriptions of aspects of the mind, as instincts, conscience, and self-analytical thought are given. Mishra emphasizes practice and experience, rather than philosophical theories only, to aid the individual aspiring to self-realization.

II. Conclusions

(1) As presented in the Brahma-Sūtra, no final definition of spiritual freedom can be stated. While Bādarāyaṇa writes that spiritual freedom is found in oneness with Brahman, this can be interpreted in several ways, as the differing opinions of Śaṅkara, Rāmānuja, and Madhva attest.

The commentators have in common an acceptance of the Vedas as valid spiritual authority, belief in Brahman as an absolute reality and as creator of the universe. In regard to spiritual freedom, however, Śaṅkara felt it meant total non-duality with Brahman; for Rāmānuja it was non-duality with qualifications; and for Madhva, Brahman and man must remain eternally separate.

These differences are at once a handicap and a strength. While no final definitive statement can be made, commentators have been free to develop their own line of thinking with some flexibility, thus granting expression to different temperaments and levels of understanding. The followers of Śaṅkara, for instance, have often emphasized intellectual understanding, while those of Rāmānuja and Madhva stress a theistic devotion to God. Both have validity, and both find support in the Brahma-Sūtra. As Radhakrishnan states, Śaṅkara and Rāmānuja represent uninterrupted traditions in Indian thought. To his mind, their ideas are not exclusive of each other but are complimentary.[1] It is as if each were viewing a scene from different windows, and so have different perspectives of the same facts.

(2) The Brahma-Sūtra is clear in its statements that right knowledge is necessary for realization of spiritual freedom. The commentators all agree in this. Indeed, right knowledge of Brahman is liberation. Academic learning is not implied, but rather an intuitive and wholistic understanding. This right knowledge cannot be directly caused. However, by purification of the mind, selfless service, and meditation on the supreme being, right knowledge can occur.

(3) With regard to spiritual freedom, the Īśa and Kena Upaniṣads were seen to be identical in scope and purpose with the Brahma-Sūtra. Oneness with God, removal of ignorance, and realization of right knowledge are suggested as definitions. Liberation is not achieved by mental activity nor by willpower; man must serve in the

---

[1]S. Radhakrishnan, The Brahma-Sūtra: The Philosophy of Spiritual Life (London: George Allen & Unwin Ltd., 1960), p. 51.

world without thought of reward as well as realizing that his mind and all manifestation are one with God.

(4) The concept of spiritual freedom as found in the tradition of the Brahma-Sūtra was seen to be expressed in modern terms through the work of Dr. Rammurti S. Mishra. His interpretation of man's essential non-duality with Brahman is the same as Śaṅkara's. One of Mishra's contributions has been to adapt current psychological techniques and analysis of experience toward realization of non-dualistic right knowledge. Thus the ideas embodied in the sūtras can be put to practical use today. He discusses the purification of cittam by means of meditation, use of nādam (inner sound current), the eight steps of yoga, devotion, and self-analysis. While the Brahma-Sūtra mentions types of spiritual practices, its focus is basically philosophical rather than pragmatic.

Mishra also suggests that the Sāṅkhya dualism may be reconciled with Vedānta as espoused in the Brahma-Sūtra by postulating that puruṣa (consciousness) and prakṛti (nature) depend ultimately on Brahman. Thus an integration is presented of the arguments between Vedānta and Sāṅkhya found in the first two chapters of the Brahma-Sūtra.

Many other leaders are involved today in psycho-spiritual disciplines. There is great value in linking an ancient, revered system of thought with modern insight. More research into other modern philosophers, in light of the Brahma-Sūtra, could further clarify our views and put them in historic and philosophic perspective.

The Brahma-Sūtra, while not widely known in the west, offers a valuable reference for this sort of study. It summarizes and expresses several major interpretations of spiritual freedom, harmonizes a number of philosophic differences, and offers some practical suggestions for spiritual practice.

Academic curiosity is not the only reason for this kind of investigation. If we are committed to the evolvement of man to higher levels of awareness, then it is necessary to look at what great sages of the centuries have written as well as where we are today in this search. One's entire attitude toward life is implicated. As Gandhi stated, if we truly realize our identity with God and each other, then our life will be devoted to service and renunciation. Nothing can belong to us personally; all ignorance and suffering loses its sense of reality when we become aware that all is Brahman.

SELECTED BIBLIOGRAPHY

A. Books

Akhilananda, Swami. Hindu Psychology: Its Meaning for the West. London: Routledge & Kegan Paul Ltd., 1960.

Aurobindo, Sri. Isha Upanishad. Pondicherry: Sri Aurobindo Ashram, 1973.

________. Kena Upanishad. Pondicherry: Sri Aurobindo Ashram, 1970.

________. The Life Divine. 2 vols. Pondicherry: Sri Aurobindo Ashram, 1973.

________. On the Veda. Pondicherry: Sri Aurobindo Ashram, 1964.

________. The Synthesis of Yoga. Pondicherry: Sri Aurobindo Ashram, 1971.

Burtt, Edwin A. Types of Religious Philosophy. Revised ed. New York: Harper & Brothers, 1951.

Campbell, Joseph. The Mythic Image. New Jersey: Princeton University Press, 1974.

Chatterjee, Satischandra, and Dhirendramohan Datta. An Introduction to Indian Philosophy. Calcutta: University of Calcutta, 1968.

Chaudhuri, Haridas. Being, Evolution and Immortality: An Outline of Integral Philosophy. Wheaton, Ill.: The Theosophical Publishing House, 1974.

________. Integral Yoga: The Concept of Harmonious and Creative Living. San Francisco: California Institute of Asian Studies, 1965.

________. Philosophy of Meditation. 2nd ed. San Francisco: Cultural Integration Fellowship, Inc., 1974.

Davis, Roy Eugene. The Bhagavad-Gita: God's Revealing Word. Georgia: CSA Press, 1968.

________. This Is Reality. Georgia: CSA Press, 1962.

Evans-Wentz, W. Y., ed. The Tibetan Book of the Great Liberation or the Method of Realizing Nirvana Through Knowing the Mind. London: Oxford University Press, 1968.

Gambhirananda, Swami, trans. Brahma-Sūtra Bhāṣya of Śaṅkarācārya, by Śrī Śankarācārya. Calcutta: Advaita Ashrama, 1972.

Iyer, M. K. V. Advaita Vedānta. Bombay: Asia Publishing House, 1964.

Johnson, Clive, ed. Vedanta: An Anthology of Hindu Scripture, Commentary, and Poetry. New York: Harper & Row, 1971.

Jung, Carl G. Memories, Dreams, Reflections. New York: Random House, 1961.

Krishnamurti, J. Beginnings of Learning. New York: Harper & Row, 1975.

________. Freedom from the Known. New York: Harper & Row, 1969.

________. The Impossible Question. New York: Harper & Row, 1972.

________. The Only Revolution. New York: Harper & Row, 1970.

Lal, Chaman, ed. Yoga of Meditation. Florida: Chaman Lal, 1971.

MacDonell, Arthur Anthony. A Vedic Reader for Students. Madras: Oxford University Press, 1970.

Madhavananda, Swami, trans. Vivekachūḍāmaṇi, by Śrī Śankarācārya. Calcutta: Advaita Ashrama, 1970.

Maitra, Sushil K., and others. Radhakrishnan: Comparative Studies in Philosophy. London: George Allen & Unwin Ltd., 1951.

Mishra, Rammurti S. Fundamentals of Yoga: A Handbook of Theory, Practice, and Application. New York: The Julian Press, 1959.

________. Isha Upanishad. Dayton, Ohio: Yoga Society, 1962.

________. Kena Upanishad. Syracuse, N.Y.: Yoga Society, 1963.

________. The Textbook of Yoga Psychology: A New Translation and Interpretation of Patanjali's Yoga Sutras for Meaningful Application in all Modern Psychological Disciplines. New York: The Julian Press, Inc., 1963.

Monier-Williams, Monier. A Sanskrit-English Dictionary: Etymologically and Philologically Arranged with Special Reference to Cognate Indo-European Languages. Oxford: Clarendon Press, 1970.

Moore, Charles A., ed. The Indian Mind: Essentials of Indian Philosophy and Culture. Honolulu: University of Hawaii Press, 1967.

Muktananda, Swami. Guru: Chitshaktivilas, the Play of Consciousness. New York: Harper & Row, 1971.

Needleman, Jacob. The New Religions. New York: Doubleday & Company, 1970.

Nikhilananda, Swami, trans. Atmabodha by Śrī Śaṅkarācārya. Madras: Sri Ramakrishna Math, 1967.

Nityaswarupananda, Swami, trans. Aṣṭāvakra Saṁhitā. Calcutta: Advaita Ashrama, 1969.

Osborne, Arthur, ed. The Teachings of Ramana Maharshi in His Own Words. New York: Samuel Weiser, Inc., 1971.

Prabhavananda, Swami, and Christopher Isherwood. How to Know God: the Yoga Aphorisms of Patanjali. Hollywood, California: Vedanta Press, 1953.

Radhakrishnan, Sarvepalli. Indian Philosophy. 2 vols. New York: The Macmillan Company, 1962.

________. The Principal Upaniṣads. London: George Allen & Unwin Ltd., 1969.

________, trans. The Brahma-Sūtra: The Philosophy of Spiritual Life by Bādarāyaṇa. London: George Allen & Unwin Ltd., 1960.

________, and Charles A. Moore. Indian Philosophy. New Jersey: Princeton University Press, 1957.

Ramakrishna, Sri. Teachings of Sri Ramakrishna. Calcutta: Advaita Ashrama, 1967.

Ramana Maharishi, Bhagavan Sri. Maharshi's Gospel: Book I and II, Being Answers of Bhagavan Sri Ramana Maharshi to Questions Put to Him by Several Devotees. 2 vols. Tiruvannamali: Sri Ramanashram, 1946.

Ramdas, Swami. God-Experience, ed. K.M. Munshi and R.R. Diwakar. Bombay: Bharatiya Vidya Bhavan, 1969.

________. World Is God. South India: Anandashram, 1955.

Satya Sai Baba, Sri. Teachings of Sri Satya Sai Baba. Georgia: CSA Printing and Bindery, Inc., 1974.

Sharma, Chandradhar. A Critical Survey of Indian Philosophy. Delhi: Motilal Banarsidass, 1964.

Sharma, H.D. Bādarāyaṇa, Bhramasūtra-Catuhsūtri: The First Four Aphorisms of Brahmasūtras along with Śaṅkarācārya's Commentary with English Translation, Notes and Index. Poona: Oriental Book Agency, 1967.

Sircar, Mahendranath. Systems of Vedantic Thought and Culture. Calcutta: University of Calcutta, 1925.

Taimni, I.K. The Science of Yoga: The Yoga-Sūtras of Patañjali in Sanskrit with Transliteration in Roman, Translation in English and Commentary. Wheaton, Ill.: The Theosophical Publishing House, 1967.

Thibaut, George, trans. The Vedānta Sūtras of Bādarāyaṇa: With the Commentary by Śaṅkara. 2 vols. New York: Dover Publications, Inc., 1962.

Tyberg, Judith M. The Language of the Gods: Sanskrit Keys to India's Wisdom. Los Angeles: East-West Cultural Center, 1970.

Van der Post, Laurens. Jung and the Story of Our Times. New York: Pantheon Books, 1975.

Vireswarananda, Swami, trans. *Brahma-Sutras*, by Bādarāyaṇa. Calcutta: Advaita Ashrama, 1970.

Vivekananda, Swami. *Rāja-Yoga*. New York: Ramaskrishna-Vivekananda Center, 1955.

Watts, Alan W. *Psychotherapy East and West*. New York: New American Library, 1961.

Zimmer, Heinrich. *Philosophies of India*, ed. Joseph Campbell. New Jersey: Princeton University Press, 1969.

B. Periodicals

Banerjee, B. B., "The Concept of Liberation in the Vedas and Upanishads," *Calcutta Review*, 157 (1960), 110-118.

Chaudhuri, Haridas, "The Concept of Brahman in Hindu Philosophy," *Philosophy East and West*, IV, 1 (April, 1954).

Maitra, Sushil K., "Mukti and Bhakti as Highest Values," *Journal of Indian Academy of Philosophy*, II, No. 1 & 2 (1963), 14-28.

Rao, P. Nagaraja, "The Concept of Moksa," *Prabuddha Bharata*, 66 (January, 1961), 23-26.

यत्परं ब्रह्म सर्वात्मा विश्वस्यायतनं महत् ।

सूक्ष्मात्सूक्ष्मतरं नित्यं तत्त्वमेव त्वमेव तत् ॥

कैवल्योपनिषद् ॥ १६ ॥

That which is the supreme Brahman,
the self in all, the support of
the universe, subtler than the
subtle and eternal . . . that thou art;
thou art that.

Kaivalyopaniṣad 16

ओं शान्तिः । शान्तिः । शान्तिः ॥

Printed in Great Britain
by Amazon

54232359R00063